THE
MINDFULNESS
BREAKTHROUGH

SARAH SILVERTON

Foreword by Jon Kabat-Zinn

THE
MINDFULNESS
BREAKTHROUGH

The Revolutionary Approach to Dealing with Stress, Anxiety and Depression

Endorsed by
**The Centre for Mindfulness Research
and Practice, Wales, UK**

WATKINS PUBLISHING

LONDON

The Mindfulness Breakthrough
Sarah Silverton

First published in the UK and USA in 2012 by
Watkins Publishing, an imprint of Duncan Baird Publishers Ltd
Sixth Floor, Castle House
75–76 Wells Street
London W1T 3QH

Conceived, created and designed by Duncan Baird Publishers

Managing Editor: Sandra Rigby
Senior Editor: Fiona Robertson
Editor: Jane McIntosh
Managing Designer: Suzanne Tuhrim
Picture Research: Emma Copestake
Production: Uzma Taj

British Library Cataloguing-in-Publication Data:
A CIP record for this book is available from the British Library

Library of Congress Cataloging-in-Publication Data available

ISBN: 978-1-78028-107-0

10 9 8 7 6 5 4 3 2 1

Typeset in Omnes and Caslon
Colour reproduction by XY Digital
Printed in Singapore by Imago

NOTE
This book is not intended as a replacement for professional medical treatment and advice. The Publisher
and Author cannot accept responsibility for any damage incurred as a result of any of the therapeutic
methods contained in this work.

Distributed in the USA and Canada by
Sterling Publishing Co., Inc.
387 Park Avenue South
New York, NY 10016-8810

For information about custom editions, special sales, premium and corporate purchases, please contact
Sterling Special Sales Department at 800-805-5489 or specialsales@sterlingpub.com.

Contents

Foreword

At first blush, to use the word "breakthrough" in association with a book gives a sense of marketing hype. But in this case, it is actually appropriate. The breakthrough, however, is not the book itself nor the programme it describes. The breakthrough is a potential that lies within you, and each one of us, in any and every moment.

In Chinese, the ideogram for "breakthrough" is related to the ideogram for "turning", as in "to rotate," "to revolve", "to shift." What is shifting with the cultivation of greater mindfulness is your perspective on life, your sense of who you are in relationship to your own life and to others, and what is possible if you are willing to pay attention in the present moment while allowing yourself to be open-hearted and spacious. Mindfulness literally and metaphorically catalyzes a rotation in consciousness. You inhabit your life differently. This indeed can be a momentous breakthrough, affecting your health and well-being in profound ways that are increasingly being documented by scientific research.

I wish you all the best in discovering this hidden but wholly accessible dimension of your own being, as you explore this beautifully crafted book and the mindfulness practices and teachings that are skilfully laid out for you to engage in and adapt to your own life circumstances.

Jon Kabat-Zinn, PhD
Professor of Medicine emeritus, University of Massachusetts Medical School, and author of *Full Catastrophe Living* and *Coming to Our Senses*

Authors' Preface

The writers of this book have been practising mindfulness for many years. We teach and train in mindfulness through the Centre for Mindfulness Research and Practice at Bangor University, North Wales, which has offered mindfulness classes in a variety of settings throughout the UK and Europe for more than 10 years.

Some of our classes are specifically for people with a particular problem or illness – perhaps a history of depression, or a condition such as cancer. Other classes are open to anyone who has an interest in taking part in the mindfulness programme. Throughout the book you will find stories that people coming to our classes over the years have told us about their experience of mindfulness. (We have changed some details to be sure that each person's privacy is protected.)

Mindfulness is an approach that has been found through research to be helpful for people with many different specific conditions, such as depression, anxiety, chronic pain and chronic fatigue – to name just a few – but most importantly it is helpful for all of us because we are human. As such, we may struggle with life and all the challenges it brings. Mindfulness can help us to live our lives fully, with increased skill, ease and flexibility. We hope that this book will help introduce you to mindfulness, both from a theoretical perspective and through actual experience. Mindfulness can help us to discover things about ourselves, and from that knowledge find ways to change the way we live our lives.

Practising mindfulness is an essential aspect of learning about mindfulness – just understanding the theory doesn't give us a full appreciation of all its layers. There are exercises in this book to give you a taste of mindful awareness, but we strongly recommend that you attend a class with an experienced mindfulness teacher. CDs are available to use alongside this book, but the support of a class, if there is one in your area, is really the best way to explore how mindfulness can be beneficial in your life (see page 178 for how to find mindfulness classes near you).

Mindfulness practice isn't appropriate for everyone, and you may find that it is not suitable for your stage of life right now. Mindfulness invites us to turn our attention toward our experience, including its more challenging aspects, so if you are receiving counselling or medical treatment, it is especially important to seek professional advice before you begin mindfulness practice.

Part I

Understanding Mindfulness

Being mindful,
we are waking up
to what our senses
are telling us.

01.

Introducing Mindfulness

By Sarah Silverton

When we are being mindful, we are choosing to notice the details of our experiences, just as they are in this moment and without judging or trying to change them in the first instance.

The Development of Mindfulness

Mindfulness meditation has developed over 2,500 years. Its roots are found in Eastern philosophy, but in the Western world it has been growing fast and is now becoming a mainstream and recommended secular or non-religious approach found in health care, social care, education and business settings.

Ideas that are central to mindfulness programmes today can be found in early Buddhist teachings, and arise from an understanding that all human beings experience their world in certain ways.

- As humans we all have the experience of finding aspects of ourselves or our lives unsatisfactory in some way. Things are sometimes not exactly how we want them to be, and this is an expected and natural part of life.
- When this is the case, it is human nature to want to seek change. We sometimes use a lot of energy to push against, fight with, resist or move away from our current experiences. Alternatively, if we like our experience, we will try to hold on to it and retain the *status quo* for as long as possible. When things are neither unsatisfactory nor just how we want them to be, we tend to tune out from these experiences and not notice them.
- As we practise mindfulness we discover and come to know deeply that these human tendencies can actually create distress in our lives; and instead of believing that external events alone are the cause of our distress and unhappiness, we start to see the role that each of us plays through our reactions to events.
- We can then make choices about how we approach our life experiences and how we act in our life. Choosing to be awake to our experience through mindful awareness can really help us with this.

The principles of mindfulness are known in Buddhism as the Four Noble Truths. Originating from the Buddha, they have been successfully woven into programmes to teach mindfulness to people in the West. It is important to emphasize that if you choose to learn about mindfulness this doesn't mean that you need to be a Buddhist. These ideas just offer an understanding of ways that we create and can respond to struggle and suffering in our lives.

Mindfulness invites us to notice our natural tendency to relate to our experience in automatic ways. It encourages us to explore the possibility of not reacting purely out of habit. Practising mindfulness teaches us to see things clearly and to develop skills in choosing a response to situations in our lives where we find ourselves pushing against, fighting with, or clinging onto something.

Mindfulness-Based Stress Reduction (MBSR)

In the 1970s Jon Kabat-Zinn, a molecular biologist with a Buddhist meditation background, began to develop and deliver a non-religious version of meditation. From 1979 his Stress Reduction and Relaxation Programme of eight weekly classes for medical patients (later to become known as MBSR) was offered in the hospital at the University of Massachusetts Medical Center in Worcester, Massachusetts, to individuals with a wide range of chronic health conditions. Having tried the available medical interventions, these people hadn't been "cured", and so were left with the prospect of no further treatment and having to manage their chronic symptoms in their bodies and lives as best they could.

Many of us have a lot of faith in the medical profession to fix our physical and mental health problems. We expect that someone else can make us completely better, and often our own role in this process is not central. However, Kabat-Zinn offered a radically different approach where there was no "fix" or cure on offer; instead it was the patients themselves who were looking at the details of their difficult circumstances and finding new ways to respond to their conditions.

He developed a programme where people attended a two-hour class once a week for eight weeks. Between classes, people were asked to practise mindfulness in their lives on a daily basis at home. The participants were experiencing many different conditions, such as chronic pain, heart problems, arthritis, cancer, anxiety and psoriasis. Because it was impossible in the classes to address each of these conditions separately, Kabat-Zinn explored the *shared nature of human distress*, rather than its external trigger. The group supported each other in the active investigation of experiences arising moment by moment – experiences related not just to their particular conditions but also to other aspects of their lives. Jon's message to participants was that there is "more right with you than wrong with you". He pointed out that we so often focus on what's wrong, needs changing and should be different in our lives, that we let this dominate and miss the many aspects of our experience that are pleasurable, satisfying and "right".

Kabat-Zinn and his colleagues at the Center for Mindfulness in Medicine, Health Care, and Society have continued to deliver classes in MBSR, to train others to teach this approach throughout the world and to carry out research.

Other approaches have grown out of the firm foundations of MBSR. These have often combined the mindfulness approach with other types of therapy, or adapted the programme to be delivered to people with specific needs.

Mindfulness-Based Cognitive Therapy (MBCT)

Mindfulness-Based Cognitive Therapy was adapted directly from MBSR, but it also includes ideas and practices from Cognitive Behavioural Therapy (CBT). Developed in the UK and Canada by leading CBT therapists Mark Williams (Bangor and then Oxford University), John Teasdale (Cambridge University)

There is more right with you than wrong with you.

Jon Kabat-Zinn

MBSR
has been adapted
for other health
problems.

MBCT
has been adapted for
other health problems
such as cancer and
chronic fatigue.

MBCT
can also be
offered to a mixed,
general public
group.

MBSR
Other mindfulness-
based approaches
have developed
out of MBSR.

MBCT
(Mindfulness-based
Cognitive Therapy)
for depression relapse
prevention (2000) was
given NICE guideline
approval in 2010 (UK).

**ACT
and DBT**
Acceptance
and Commitment
Therapy and Dialectical
Behavioural Therapy.

MBSR
(Mindfulness-Based
Stress Reduction) was
developed to help clients
who were experiencing
a range of different
health conditions.

**BUDDHIST
TEACHING**
Mindfulness-based approaches
have developed from Buddhist
teachings, which originated around
500 BC. With its roots in Buddhism,
mindfulness has a number of
branches, the main ones
being MBSR and MBCT.

and Zindel Segal (University of Toronto), it was intended specifically as a treatment programme for people with a history of recurrent depression to help them stay well. At that time (in the early 1990s) recurrent depression was almost always treated with anti-depressant medication so a psychological approach to relapse prevention was a new development.

Cognitive Behavioural Therapy was already known to help people with acute depressive illness. Being familiar with the work of Kabat-Zinn, Segal, Teasdale and Williams explored how CBT and mindfulness might be included in their new programme for relapse prevention. The result was a combination of both approaches, but predominantly mindfulness, retaining much of the structure and intentions of MBSR (albeit tailored for the chosen client group).

Segal, Teasdale and Williams carried out research from 1995 to 1999, and concluded that MBCT approximately halved the likelihood of depression recurring in cases where the participants had three or more previous episodes. These results were replicated by Teasdale and Helen Ma in 2002.

Mindfulness-Based Cognitive Therapy now has a firm and growing evidence base, and in 2010 was recommended in the UK by the National Institute for Health and Clinical Excellence (NICE) guidelines as the treatment of choice for recurrent depressive illness. In 2010 Willem Kuyken, Professor of Clinical Psychology and Co-Founder of the Mood Disorders Centre at the University of Exeter, found that when people meet the criteria for MBCT and the classes are offered by teachers with appropriate MBCT training, this appears to be a significant alternative to anti-depressant medication. (See also page 178.)

Mindfulness-Based Cognitive Therapy has since been adapted by others such as Trish Bartley (Centre for Mindfulness Research and Practice) and Christina Surawy (Oxford Mindfulness Centre) for people with cancer and chronic fatigue. Mindfulness is central to many therapeutic techniques including Acceptance and Commitment Therapy, Dialectical Behavioural Therapy and Mindfulness-Based Relapse Prevention. Mindfulness-based approaches continue to grow and evolve.

The Mindfulness Experience

Being mindful is actually something that we all did very naturally when we were small children. When we are being mindful, we are choosing to notice the details of our experiences, just as they are in this moment and without judging or trying to change them in the first instance. Sometimes mindfulness is described as seeing clearly.

If you watch young children or animals exploring their world, you will see that they are curious, fully absorbed in the present moment, engaged in their activities and playful in their exploration. Experiences are new, fascinating and rich in possibility. This attitude and kind of attention is what we aim to rekindle in ourselves as adults through mindfulness practice. We will learn to develop our curiosity and ability to notice a wide range of experiences both within and around us. We will turn toward the many experiences of being in this moment.

As adults we have been trained to analyze and make sense of our experience, mostly by thinking about it. We aren't encouraged to play or to explore or to really experience our world. Once the mind has labelled and understood an experience conceptually, that's considered enough.

Being mindful, we are waking up to what our senses are telling us. Our minds and bodies constantly receive information, refreshing it moment by moment. This happens automatically and without any effort on our part. Mindfulness invites us to reconnect to this information, using our senses of sight, sound, smell, taste and touch. When we're being mindful we can choose to pay attention to each and every experience. We become awake to our experience of ourselves in our lives.

Layers of Experiencing

The diagram below shows how we receive and tend to respond to experience. The centre is where incoming sensations directly affect our physical body and our emotions. This is the stable core that we return to in mindfulness practice when we need to reconnect and pay attention to what is happening in this moment.

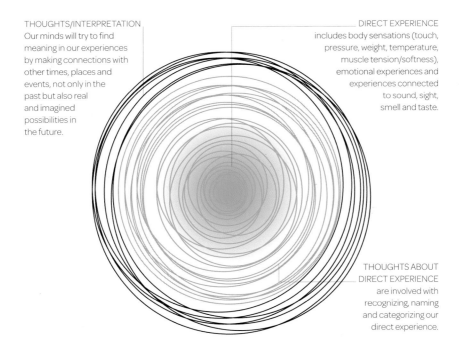

THOUGHTS/INTERPRETATION
Our minds will try to find meaning in our experiences by making connections with other times, places and events, not only in the past but also real and imagined possibilities in the future.

DIRECT EXPERIENCE
includes body sensations (touch, pressure, weight, temperature, muscle tension/softness), emotional experiences and experiences connected to sound, sight, smell and taste.

THOUGHTS ABOUT DIRECT EXPERIENCE
are involved with recognizing, naming and categorizing our direct experience.

As we experience mindfulness we recognize three layers of experiencing. Often our minds move us quickly to the conceptual outer ring of thoughts about meaning and associations. Mindfulness lets us see how our mind builds on our direct experience with labels and stories. These can take us far from our direct experience and we can become disconnected from actual, direct experience in the present moment. Mindfulness helps us to keep the steady core of direct experience.

Exercise: Tuning in to Sitting

You are now invited to practise mindfulness by tuning in to your experience just as it is at this moment. You are going to spend five minutes simply noticing whatever you notice about your experience of sitting.

1 Notice the sensations as you sit here – your feet making contact with the floor, your bottom on the seat of the chair or on the cushion. Is there any feeling of pressure, or perhaps hardness or softness?

2 Can you feel any difference in temperature between your body parts and the various surfaces they are touching?

3 Does your body feel large or small compared to the chair you are sitting on?

4 Can you hear anything? What are the different sounds that you notice around you?

5 What else do you notice as you sit here for a few more moments?

6 There is no need to change your experience in any way – just notice.

Sometimes mindfulness is described as seeing clearly.

Mindfulness and the Brain

Neuroscience research over recent years has led to understanding that the human brain can change in both structure and activity (known as neuroplasticity) and that this change is directly connected to how we use our brain.

A number of neuroscience studies have specifically involved mindfulness meditators. In 2003, Richard Davidson, Jon Kabat-Zinn and their colleagues found that people trained to meditate by taking part in the eight-week Mindfulness-Based Stress Reduction programme showed important changes in brain activation in the prefrontal cortex.

A shift from right-sided activation to more left-sided activation in key areas of the brain associated with emotion regulation was found, suggesting an increase in ability to deal with situations in a more positive and balanced way. The changes found were still evident when people were tested again four months later. This important study also connected the changes in activation in these areas of the brain to a stronger immune response in the meditators studied (following a "flu" vaccine given at the end of the MBSR training).

Sara Lazar's 2005 study of experienced meditators found changes in the thickness of the cerebral cortex, with thickness in some areas equivalent to that expected in people 20 years younger. This suggests that there may be a slowing down in experienced meditators of the natural thinning that happens in some areas of the brain as we age. Britta Holzel, Sara Lazar and their colleagues (2009, 2010 and 2011) have added further to the growing understanding of the effects of meditation on the brain, and of what this means in our lives. Other changes include thickening in the hippocampus and thinning in the amygdala.

This evidence suggests that learning to meditate can alter both the structure and activity of our brains, and that these changes positively affect our well-being. This is very encouraging.

While there are still many questions regarding the details of such changes and how the various areas of the brain interrelate, these studies are very encouraging. The areas of the brain that are linked to helping us regulate our emotions seem to be particularly influenced by meditation practice.

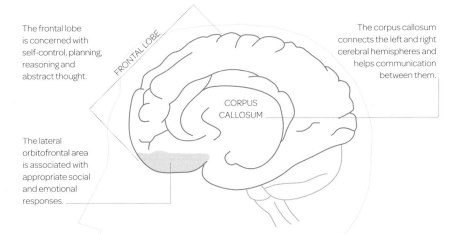

The frontal lobe is concerned with self-control, planning, reasoning and abstract thought.

FRONTAL LOBE

The corpus callosum connects the left and right cerebral hemispheres and helps communication between them.

CORPUS CALLOSUM

The lateral orbitofrontal area is associated with appropriate social and emotional responses.

Mind–Body Connections

In the West we have traditionally viewed the mind and body to be separate (in contrast to the more holistic approach of Eastern countries). Medical services clearly reflect this, with a number of different medical specialisms and doctors who have expertise in only one organ of the body. There has been very little focus on how our body and mind interrelate or function as a whole.

A few studies show interesting ways in which the body and mind may influence each other. In one, patients being treated for psoriasis found that mindfulness practice, used in addition to the standard light treatment offered for this condition, helped their skin heal more quickly. Another study has found that when people are more closely informed and involved in their medical treatment, they get well more quickly. How we feel about the physical environment in which we are treated has also been found to influence how quickly we recover.

Mindfulness in Everyday Life

Mindfulness offers a way of understanding both the joy and the inherent difficulty of being human. As we live our lives in this body/mind that evolution has shaped, mindfulness allows us to respond skilfully to habitual tendencies, and live our lives more fully and with greater ease.

As human beings we have much in common, but we are also individuals, with different experiences, behaviours and attitudes. Mindfulness offers a path that meets us just as we are, helping us to find our own way.

Mindfulness Stories

Matthew worked extremely hard in order to afford things that he thought would bring him happiness. When he managed to acquire them he couldn't understand why they didn't make him happy, and he worked even harder to buy more. To his surprise, he discovered through practising mindfulness that there were many things about his life – just as it was in that moment – which were perfect. Mindful awareness allowed him to begin to appreciate what he already had.

Ellen had suffered from chronic fatigue for many years. She was the mother of two children and worked hard to show herself and others that she could cope and was in control. Mindfulness practice taught her to pay attention to what her body was telling her. As she listened, she discovered that she could skilfully respond to her tiredness by resting for a while when she began to feel fatigued. She found that this seemed to offer her more reliable energy. Also she found that she gained great pleasure from *being with* her children rather than just *doing things* for them.

Joe had chronic pain from a back injury. He had dealt with this by curbing his activities in order to reduce the possibility of experiencing further injury and pain. His life had become restricted and unrewarding. He discovered through mindfulness that he could explore his pain, become familiar with it and recognize its patterns. This allowed him increasingly to meet his pain gently rather than brace himself and fight its very existence in his life. In really getting to know his pain, he could then choose how to respond. He was surprised to find that, even as he re-engaged in the activities of his life, his experience of pain decreased.

Henry was a carer for his wife who had multiple sclerosis (MS). She had been ill for a long time and his life was taken up with looking after her and in managing the house. He found through his mindfulness practice that he could notice and really savour the beautiful moments that still existed in their lives, despite her illness. He found that he could reconnect with his wife as a person rather than as an MS sufferer. He could take time to see sunsets and the birds in their garden, and create opportunities for them both to enjoy music and the sunshine. He said that he stopped waiting to live his life and decided to live it anyway.

Fiona had experienced a difficult childhood. She had undergone lots of therapy over the years to help her understand why she felt sad for much of the time. Mindfulness practice allowed her to see the amount of time that she spent remembering the past and how it had made her unhappy. Learning to focus on how things were in her present moments helped her to let go of the thoughts that had dominated her existence. She began to live her life in the here-and-now. When memories appeared she was able to recognize them, but then reconnect to the reality of her current experience and see that things in her life were actually fine in the present.

Savour the surprising and beautiful moments in life, despite the problems you may face.

The Benefits of Mindfulness

The following are some ways in which mindfulness has been acknowledged to support us:

CONNECTION

Mindfulness can help us to feel a greater connection with ourselves, and with experiences in our bodies and our minds. We can also feel more connected to those around us and to the world that we live in.

PERSPECTIVE

We can stand back and see things more clearly. Mindfulness helps us to look at the "bigger picture" of experience, which includes what's *right* as well as the problems in life. It can open us to pleasurable experiences, perhaps offering us a more balanced view of how life is, moment by moment. We may also recognize that difficulties can arise from our own reactions, rather than being the result of external forces (and therefore out of our control).

CHOICE

We can have more choice about where to place our focus of attention, and learn to open up and be receptive to the information this presents. Mindfulness also increases our repertoire of ways we can manage difficulties in our lives, giving us a greater range of choices about how to act. We learn how to respond wisely to what we find, rather than reacting habitually. Choice can also give us a greater sense of control over our lives and reduce our reliance on others.

SELF-KNOWLEDGE

As we practise mindfulness, we spend a lot of time noticing and becoming familiar with all our experiences – including the difficult things in life – and learn to recognize how the different aspects interconnect. We learn a lot about our patterns and habits.

The depth and detail of experience, that is both known through our thoughts but also known through our felt experience, can greatly add to our understanding. We can see how experience continually changes and unfolds over time.

KINDNESS/SELF-COMPASSION

Learning to care for ourselves is a very important aspect of mindfulness. Learning to value ourselves and to respond to ourselves with kindness is often something that people find difficult to do.

Through practising mindfulness, we learn to take care of ourselves when times are difficult and we are in pain. We can see when we are being self-critical and can feel the impact of this. We learn that we can be kind instead. As we become more in tune with our experience, we develop the ability to choose activities in our lives that nourish us and to do fewer of the ones that deplete us.

CHANGING MENTAL GEARS

Neurologically, it appears that mindfulness allows us to engage a different "mental gear" – one in which we can see clearly how things are *now* – and find appropriate and creative responses that are relevant and helpful.

It may already be clear that mindfulness is not simply a technique that can help people who have specific conditions to manage their symptoms. Indeed, mindfulness is much more *a way of living* – that is, a choice which is available to all human beings.

Mindfulness is an approach that we learn over time and with practice, so that we may have skills available to us not only when life is difficult for whatever reason (as will inevitably be the case for all of us at some point in our lives), but also – importantly – when life is good, allowing us to engage fully in the moment and in living our lives.

02.

Paying Attention
Mindfully

By Sarah Silverton

Mindfulness lets us choose where to focus our attention, opening ourselves to the details of our rich and changing experience.

Turning Our Attention Toward Our Experience

When we begin to practise mindfulness, it often comes as a surprise to find that our minds are usually somewhere other than in the present moment. We frequently spend our time thinking about the future: what we are going to be doing next, planning or anticipating events, maybe even worrying.

Or we may think about the past, remembering and processing experiences that have already happened to us. This is what the mind does – it's perfectly normal – but it means that we often miss the experience of being here in this moment.

Acting on Autopilot

Maybe you know what it's like to drive somewhere and have little memory of the journey, or perhaps read a book and find you have turned the pages without knowing what you've been reading? Importantly, we often can't bring to mind the thoughts that we've been having during these times. On such occasions we are not making a choice about where our minds go and are operating on "autopilot".

In our busy lives we are actively encouraged to multi-task and we develop the ability to do many different things at the same time. For example, we may eat our breakfast while we're packing bags for work or school, listening to the radio, talking to family members or reading a newspaper. Our attention is so divided that we only catch glimpses of each of these activities – so much of our activity happens through sheer force of *habit*.

Our mind's ability to be on autopilot is, in fact, essential as it allows us to cope with all sorts of incoming information and manage the complex and routine tasks in our lives.

When we learn to drive a car, initially we feel as if we need 10 arms and legs, but over time we learn to perform all the movements to control the vehicle safely without consciously having to think about every action. It's necessary for the mind to be able to "*habituate*", but often we move into this mode of relating to the activities and experiences in our lives without actually choosing to.

Mindfulness lets us choose where to focus our attention, opening ourselves to details of experience that we may have missed for years.

As we learn to be mindful, we are giving ourselves the *choice* to place our focus of attention where we want it to be. We can still operate on autopilot, but we can also shift mental gears when we want to. Instead of the horses being in control of the carriage, we learn to take back the reins to steer whenever that is what's needed.

When we are operating on autopilot, we tend to react habitually without access to the fuller picture. But by noticing all the detail around us at any given time, we can avail ourselves of a greater range of choices when it comes to dealing with our experience.

Our habitual patterns of behaviour can also cause us problems. These habits may be outmoded, but because of their automatic nature we are unaware of this fact. Think of it as wearing clothes that you've long outgrown!

Thinking Habits

From the moment you are born you learn to adapt the way you behave in order to meet your body and mind's needs and, thereby, ultimately remain alive. You learn to relate to the world and the important people in it so that you can be fed, and kept warm, protected and safe. This is an active process within each of us and we humans learn quickly what we have to do to get these needs met by others. We learn to act in a certain way and play by the "rules". For example:

- Doing things perfectly.
- Being strong and not showing our feelings or vulnerability.
- Trying hard at everything we do.
- Attempting to please other people, especially above pleasing ourselves.

Do you recognize any of these traits in yourself? Have you ever noticed what happens when you "disobey" these rules? (They are often so deep-rooted, they can be very hard to break.)

If we are unaware of these thinking habits, they may drive our behaviours in a way that makes us feel stuck in unhelpful patterns of action and relationships with others in our lives. On the other hand, becoming awake to our mind's activity can be very liberating, opening up endless new avenues of possibility.

Habits of the Body

We also have many habits that relate to our bodies. We may hold tension in certain places such as our shoulders, foreheads or stomachs. Sometimes we become aware of this but often it only becomes apparent after a long time when our bodies are complaining loudly. Neck and back problems are common, as is irritable bowel syndrome (IBS), connected to long-standing tension in the body.

We often stop paying any attention to the messages our body gives us, or ignore them when we do notice. Even basic messages such as being thirsty or needing to go to the toilet can be put aside in the midst of our hectic lives.

On the occasions when we listen to our bodies, we may respond in ways that seem helpful in the short term. However, often we aren't dealing with the difficulty as well as we might. Do a few glasses of wine or collapsing on the sofa in front of the TV after a stressful day at work sound familiar? These solutions may feel like they're doing some good at the time but often they don't quite match the physical or emotional need your body is highlighting.

We can also be very skilful at tuning out from these bodily messages by distracting ourselves. We often choose not to listen to what our body is telling us.

Our bodies are wise and can give us very detailed information about how we are feeling (both physically and emotionally), as well as what we need at any given moment. By reconnecting with this information, we can respond quickly and appropriately to our needs. Mindfulness allows us to do this.

Body Tension

We tend to hold a lot of tension in our head, neck, shoulders, abdomen and lower back, resulting in stiffness and pain. Mindfulness can help us to notice where tension is occurring in the body so that we can then respond in the most appropriate ways.

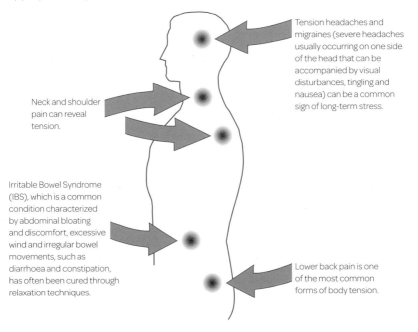

Tension headaches and migraines (severe headaches usually occurring on one side of the head that can be accompanied by visual disturbances, tingling and nausea) can be a common sign of long-term stress.

Neck and shoulder pain can reveal tension.

Irritable Bowel Syndrome (IBS), which is a common condition characterized by abdominal bloating and discomfort, excessive wind and irregular bowel movements, such as diarrhoea and constipation, has often been cured through relaxation techniques.

Lower back pain is one of the most common forms of body tension.

Doing and Being Modes of the Mind

Are you someone who writes lists to help you remember all the jobs or chores you have to do? Do you find yourself thinking and worrying about things that need to be done?

Many of us are incredibly busy, engaging in a multitude of activities, tasks and chores, and fulfilling commitments in our lives from the minute we wake up until the moment we go to bed. We constantly make lists, such as:

Feed the cat
Put out the rubbish
Pay the bills
Buy the food
Feed the family
Do the housework
Go to work ... and all the things that this entails!

"Doing mind" allows us to stay focused on completing tasks. It keeps us on track so that we keep in mind our end goal and continue until that is achieved. If we are travelling somewhere, our mind will keep the chosen destination "stored" until we get there – at that point the doing mind will refocus on the next job. Clearly, without the mind's ability to do this, getting through the complexities of the day would be very difficult; we might find ourselves half-dressed, lost on our way to work or with supper burnt in the oven!

Doing mind is very important, but mindful awareness allows us to realize that we are sometimes using this mode of mind unhelpfully. As we are focused on achieving our goal, we can miss many details of our experience in this moment – some which may be very helpful to notice.

It is our "being mind" that allows us to explore and be present with details of our experience, either when we are still or when we are doing something. Someone swimming for fitness, for example, might be using their doing mind to count the lengths that they had swum and keep an eye on the time, alert to achieving the required number at the right pace. If the same swimmer was using their being mind, they would experience the swimming itself, noticing the feel of their body as it moved through the water, seeing and hearing what was going on around them.

We can engage our doing mind when it is maybe not the most appropriate mode to be operating in. We find ourselves being busy and *doing* when this isn't needed. We can feel driven and find it hard to switch off because our doing mind keeps telling us that the job isn't completed yet. Becoming aware of which mode of mind we are using through mindfulness practice allows us the choice to switch to the mode most suited to the task.

Richard liked to go walking in the beautiful park behind his home. He chose this activity as a way of reducing his stress levels after busy periods at work. He was surprised and concerned that often he didn't feel relaxed or refreshed by his walks. A few weeks after beginning to practise mindfulness, he came to the class and was excited to report an important discovery. He had realized that he had been going for a walk in order to get his walk *done*: it had become just another task to complete. He noticed that he was very focused on getting back home and the jobs that were waiting for him there. He also noticed that as he walked, he found himself thinking about work and repeatedly mulling over the same problems. He had been so focused on these thoughts that he hadn't even seen the trees and the spring flowers. He hadn't seen the wildlife, or the dogs playing, and he hadn't noticed the people as he passed them in the park.

Using our doing mind, we may focus only on things being not as they should be, on wanting things to be different. This is evident in the Western world in the way we buy things to "improve" our lives. But these things often don't satisfy us and we just want the next thing. When we engage our doing mind with our emotional states, we may be reminded of our unhappiness, anger or fear, seeing only the gap between how we feel now and a state of happiness that we yearn for. Our doing mind will keep telling us that we are not there yet.

Richard discovered many things when he began to walk mindfully in the park:

- He could choose his walk rather than letting his habit guide his feet.
- He saw the rich details of the scenery and wildlife as he walked.
- He noticed the colour of the leaves and the smell of the damp earth.
- He heard the bird song and sounds of the wind.
- He felt the movements of his body, and could slow down or speed up depending on what his body told him.
- He could feel his feet on the ground and the air against his skin.
- He noticed the other people that passed and saw their dogs enjoying their walk and playing with sticks.

His focus on these details meant that his mind was much less drawn to memories, or to worries about work. His mind was actively exploring his experience, and because there was only so much room in his attention, other peripheral thoughts could not find the space to get established. He reported that walking in this way really did refresh him.

Being mindful and awake to our experience sounds simple, but it is actually very different from how we usually process our experience. We are trained to try constantly to improve our experience and ourselves. Mindfulness practice encourages us, as a first step, not to change what our experience is, but to see it clearly because it is already our experience, here in this moment.

Choosing Where to Place Our Attention

It may be helpful to think of your focus of attention as a beam from a torch. What you are learning to do as you practise mindfulness is to control the *direction* of the beam and the *breadth* of the beam's light.

- You will discover how to place the beam on the "object of awareness" (what you are choosing to pay attention to).
- You will find that you can narrow the beam to see precise detail or widen it to see a broader view but in less detail.
- You simply turn your beam of attention and *receive* the "image".
- The skill you are developing as you practise mindfulness is keeping the beam in the direction you choose and receiving detailed information of what is here.

Choosing a Response to Experience

As you practise mindfulness, you are learning to recognize which circumstances in your life require action and which don't, and what kind of response will be the most appropriate.

We often find that we can bring the doing mode of mind to mindfulness practice too. We notice that we have a goal in our mind as to how we are *supposed* to think or feel which is different to how things are in this moment. This can make us try too hard and be dissatisfied with what we are actually experiencing – we may feel tired and disheartened and tell ourselves, "It's a waste of time" or "I'm failing/not doing this properly" or "I'll never feel how I want to feel".

As we practise *being with* our experience, moment by moment, we develop an ability to hold our experience gently and allow things to be as they are in ourselves and the world. We learn about acceptance or letting be – acknowledging things to be as they are, which is different from passivity or resignation.

Acceptance involves us gently "holding" our experience in our awareness, long enough to see it clearly. Really seeing things as they already are can bring to awareness surprising details.

Another image that may help with understanding this concept more clearly is imagining you are with a group of toddlers or puppies. If you wanted them to come to you, what would happen if you shouted at them to come or, on the other hand, whispered quietly? It's unlikely that in either situation they would respond. But if you offered them something really interesting and encouraged them with enthusiasm and kindness to come and see, they would be much more likely to make a move – and perhaps even stay!

You can approach your own mind in the same way, as you learn to invite it to spend more time in the present moment.

Mindfulness practice is also about learning to respond to what we find. Choice becomes available when we can see our experience clearly and, based on this information, make an informed decision about how to respond most appropriately.

Gentle Curiosity

Approaching our experience gently and with kindness is a radically different way of being with ourselves.

As we actively approach our experience, whether it is pleasant or unpleasant, we are learning to allow our experience to be as it already is, rather than trying to change, fix or improve it. We are learning to look at our experience with fresh eyes and not just jump to conclusions or assume it is like it was the last time we looked. This is sometimes called the "beginner's mind".

We learn that if we pause and allow time to gather the details of our experience, we will then get a fuller picture, instead of rushing in quickly with perhaps a mismatched solution.

We learn to be patient with ourselves, our experience and the world around us. We also learn to "refresh" or update information about our present moment's experience, so we can let go of experiences that are not about now (such as worrying thoughts – in turn causing physical tension – about something that might happen in the future). We begin to notice that all experiences continually change and evolve on their own, and to question the assumption that we have to get involved and take action before any change is possible. This process of constant change is sometimes called "impermanence". Our experience continues to unfold and evolve moment by moment.

Sarah described a "revelation" while practising mindfulness. Noticing an itch on her nose, for the first time ever she didn't scratch it. When she realized that the itch went away of its own accord in only a moment or two, it was a real surprise! Up until then she had firmly believed that itches would continue forever unless they were scratched.

So now you are learning to explore, be curious about, and investigate your experience in a way that allows you to step back from it, giving you the possibility of a different perspective and more space to see your experience clearly, as it is.

Stepping
back and
seeing clearly

Choosing an
appropriate
response

Noticing
present-moment
experience

Bringing
kind and gentle
curiosity

Recognizing
and
labelling

ATTENTION

Like a lotus bud slowly unfolding,
there are many "petals" involved in our
experience that we only discover through
active attention and exploration. When we hold
an experience in our awareness and pay attention
mindfully, rather than reacting automatically,
we can see things clearly and choose an
appropriate and skilful
response.

Our experience
continues to
unfold and evolve
moment by moment.

As you practise mindfulness you are encouraging yourself to take a friendly interest in your experience, to develop an ability to take care of yourself and to respond to yourself and your circumstances kindly and wisely.

Taking care of ourselves may sound easy, but actually we often find this a very hard thing to do. We may be much more practised at taking care of people other than ourselves. Inviting ourselves to bring kindly attention to ourselves and our experience is actually quite radical.

When we speak about kindness in mindfulness we are inviting ourselves to:

- Notice the times when we are unkind to ourselves and others in our actions and thoughts.
- Allow ourselves to be us, as we are, and acknowledge that we're "good enough".
- Give ourselves encouragement.
- Recognize our achievements and qualities.
- Make space to care for ourselves in our busy lives by taking part in activities that nourish all of who we are, and which support us in living life with pleasure.
- Choose responses that will make things better, easier and more rewarding for us.
- Let go of unhelpful habits that prevent us responding appropriately and which may drain us.

03.

Practising
Mindfulness

By Sarah Silverton

This is mindfulness in practice: choosing to notice some aspect of our experience, and bringing a friendly interest to whatever we notice.

Developing Awareness of Everyday Life

The practices in this chapter are inviting you to bring mindful awareness to activities you may already do in everyday life. With all mindfulness practice it is very important that you make choices that are right for you – your body and your mind. What is right for you one day may not be wise on another day. Doing normal activities slowly can make them more challenging so please choose a speed that feels appropriate to you. Sometimes bringing attention to your breath can feel uncomfortable initially, especially if you have a history of problems with your breathing.

You are strongly encouraged to take care of yourself and never to push yourself beyond your physical or mental limits. In mindfulness practice, we always implicitly "invite" you to make a choice. It is far better to let your body and mind – if they are telling you not to do something – be the best judge of what to do, rather than slavishly follow instructions. Take your time doing your mindfulness practice, noticing whatever you notice and experiencing whatever you experience – you can't get this wrong! So let's now practise mindfulness, starting with the Eating Mindfully exercise on the following page, and see what you notice!

We talk about *practising* mindfulness because our ability to be mindful is always developing. It is really important to remember, as discussed on page 40, that when we shine the torch of our awareness, we are not *trying* to change the detail of what the light picks up; just the direction of the beam and how broadly the torch beam spreads. We are choosing the focus of our attention and the detail of our experience that we are opening our awareness to.

Exercise: Eating Mindfully

As with all the mindfulness practices we will explore in this book, it is really important that you make a *choice* as to whether to follow the invitations given in the guidance, or not. For this exercise you can choose any fruit that you have at home – it can be fresh or dried.

1 Imagine that you are seeing this thing for the very first time. You could pretend you are from another world, or maybe that you are a small child. Is it actually possible to imagine that you have never seen this object before and don't know what it is?

2 Begin to explore it with your eyes. Spend a few minutes really investigating it. What colours do you see? What is its shape? What is its texture? Do you see patterns? What size is it? If you turn it around in your fingers, does it look the same from different angles? Does the light reflect off the surface? Does it look different held up to a light? Are there details that you can notice and explore? Look again and see if there is anything that has escaped your gaze so far. Has your mind become involved in this process, naming the fruit (despite your best intentions to pretend it's an entirely new thing in your life), maybe remembering, making associations, or noticing that it looks like something else? Has your mind decided, perhaps, that it likes or dislikes this object?

3 Now explore what it feels like to touch. Is it light or heavy? Is it soft or hard? Are there parts that feel different to other parts? Is it smooth or rough, sticky or wet? What are the sensations as you hold this object in your fingers? Which fingers are touching it? Can they hold it easily without dropping it or squashing it? Do you have to decide to do this or do the body and brain manage this on their own?

CONTINUED OVERLEAF

4 When you are ready (and if you choose to), bring this object toward your face. Perhaps you notice the sensations of your hand and arm moving? If you wish, perhaps see whether it has a smell. As you breathe in its fragrance, do you notice anything happening in your body?

5 Maybe you could now touch the object with your lips to see how that feels. Is the sensation in your top and bottom lip the same?

6 Again, if you choose to and it feels right, place the object (or a bite-sized piece) in your mouth. If you like, hold it on your tongue for a few moments, feeling its weight, texture and taste. What is the experience if your tongue turns it over and moves it around your mouth?

7 When you choose to, very slowly take one bite and then pause to notice what you notice ... is there any taste, texture or moisture? Do these change moment by moment? Choose to take further bites as it feels right to do so until you are ready to start to swallow. Perhaps you will notice how many swallows are needed and the sensations as the object moves down your throat.

8 And what do you feel now? Is there still a taste or tastes in your mouth? Any moisture? Are there bits that have got stuck in your teeth?!

9 Pause to reflect on what you noticed. For example:

- What were the messages that your body/mind received about the fruit? What was most vivid: its taste, its appearance, how it felt, or its smell?
- Was there anything about the fruit that you had never noticed before?
- How busy was your mind as you explored this fruit? How easy was it to pretend that you didn't know this object? Was it surprising to notice how involved the mind can get?
- Did the intensity of your senses differ from when you usually eat this fruit? Was there anything surprising about the taste or smell?
- How different was the way you ate compared to usual? In what ways?

Below are some common observations that come up regularly among participants exploring this exercise in mindfulness classes.

- I noticed things about the piece of fruit that I had never seen before and this really surprised me.
- My senses were "sharper" somehow, so that colours, smells and tastes seemed more vivid.
- I realized that very often in everyday life I eat without paying much attention to what I am eating.
- I rarely eat without doing several other things at the same time, such as talking to family, watching television or listening to the radio, catching up on emails, reading the paper, and so on.
- How busy the mind is! It chats away constantly, getting up to all sorts of things: for example, making judgements, commenting, remembering, finding comparisons, and making sense of our experience (for example, liking or disliking).
- I noticed how my mind spends most of its time somewhere other than in the present moment.
- When I was really absorbed in what I was noticing, my mind was less busy.

Do you recognize any of these feelings from your own experience?

This is mindfulness in practice: choosing to notice some aspect of our experience, and bringing a friendly interest to whatever we notice as we place our focus of attention here. Slowing things down can help us to have time to process all the information that is available, though it isn't essential to do things slowly.

We can pay attention to our experience as we run for a bus or train in just the same way.

The Wandering Mind

Often, as we begin to practise mindfulness, we believe we are doing it wrong if the mind isn't settled on our chosen focus. As we discussed earlier, our doing mind will often conjure up some expectations of how mindfulness is supposed to be. We may expect a calm, still mind and not one that insists on thinking about work and supper, or tells us that we have something much more important – or even urgent – that needs to be done right now! This "monkey mind" that jumps around all over the place is, however, absolutely normal.

As you practise mindfulness you are learning to notice the mind's activity and then gently, but also firmly, return your attention to where you choose. You're not fixing the mind in one place or emptying it.

Paying attention mindfully is a lot like standing on one leg. If you are going to hold your balance, you will actually need to wobble around a bit! It is a dynamic process of adjusting and re-adjusting, holding the choice to be standing on one leg central in your mind. If you held your body rigidly as you balanced, you would probably fall over very quickly like a felled tree! And if your muscles were too relaxed you would slide to the ground rather than staying upright in your balance. Similarly, if you're too gentle with yourself, you may lose sight of the decision to notice your moments.

During mindfulness practice it would be very hard work (and we would most likely fail) if we tried to fix our attention and not let it wander at all – our mind is designed to think, just as our heart beats, so it *will* wander!

However, if we make no effort to place our attention where we want it to be, and give up as soon as it drifts away, it is unlikely that the mind will learn to settle and explore our experience as mindfulness invites it to.

Paying attention
mindfully is a lot like
standing on one leg.
Holding your balance
means allowing
yourself to wobble!

Investigating Bodily Sensations

The sensations in our bodies of standing, sitting, moving, digesting and breathing are always available to us as a way of being in this moment. These sensations can help us return to the here-and-now if our attention has been captured by thoughts about the past or the future, or if we find ourselves firmly in doing-mind mode – busy and driven to get tasks done. By practising being with our body sensations – tuning in to the myriad of tones, flavours, textures and colours of our experience – we can strengthen the ongoing invitation from our body to be *here*.

Your body can tell you so much about what it is to be in the present moment. It can also tell you many things about your body and your mind in that moment:

- Your body's physical needs: for example, thirst, hunger or tiredness.
- Your emotions, boredom, interest, likes and dislikes may be reflected in bodily sensations.
- Your mood can be detected in your posture.

As you practise noticing, exploring and becoming familiar with the messages your body constantly sends you, you are gathering valuable knowledge. You are accessing important resources to help you develop your skills in taking care of yourself and meeting your needs as fully as possible. So, let's see what you notice if you bring the same attitude of curiosity and "fresh, beginner's mind" as you brought to the eating practice to your experience of your body. Remember, there is *no right way to feel* – you are simply noticing whatever your experience is.

Exercise: Mindful Sitting

Choose a way to sit to practise mindfulness that will allow your body to be comfortably supported with your muscles at rest as far as possible. Whichever position you choose, you are aiming to encourage the following:

- A stable and balanced body. In a comfortable sitting posture, your body will form a firm base, from which the spine can rise through its natural curves and be at ease.
- Knees that are lower than your hips and making contact with the floor (this applies if you are sitting on a stool or cushion).
- A posture that keeps you firmly connected to the place where you are sitting.

Shaping your posture in this way makes full use of the body's natural ability to support itself, and lets it mirror your invitation to yourself to be at ease, but also awake, open and steady as you explore the experiences arising and passing, moment by moment. By listening to your body's messages, you can choose an appropriate posture for your body in this moment.

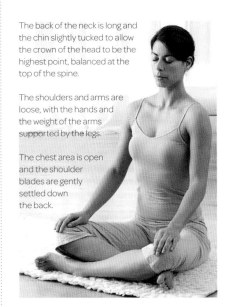

The back of the neck is long and the chin slightly tucked to allow the crown of the head to be the highest point, balanced at the top of the spine.

The shoulders and arms are loose, with the hands and the weight of the arms supported by the legs.

The chest area is open and the shoulder blades are gently settled down the back.

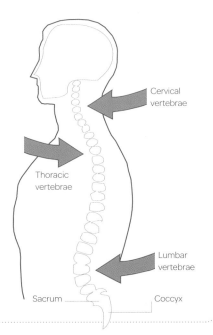

Cervical vertebrae

Thoracic vertebrae

Lumbar vertebrae

Sacrum

Coccyx

Mindfulness of Breathing

In every moment, the breath is always moving. In this way, when we are noticing our breathing, we are here, present in this moment. The breath can be like an *anchor*, holding us steadily in the present moment, when our mind and our body are reactive, unsettled or off-balance. The breath is always available to us as a place to return to in the midst of busy-ness or reactivity in our lives.

Whenever you practise mindfulness of breathing, choose to sit in the most comfortable position for your body, as it is just now. Start by tuning into the sensations that tell you that your body is sitting in this place – sensations, perhaps, of pressure, contact, weight, temperature, tingling or pulsing. You are being gently curious about whatever you find without needing things to be any particular way:

- Can you feel your feet on the floor, and your bottom on the chair?
- Can you notice sensations arising in your body – this complete body – right from the top of your head, to your fingertips and your toes?
- Do your sensations change as you explore them for a while?
- Are there some sensations that call more loudly than others, pulling your attention to them?

Staying with the Sensations of the Breath

You may find that your mind wants to get involved – it may be trying to alter or improve the breath in some way. There may be thoughts about your breathing or maybe thoughts about something quite unrelated. How would it be to just sit and allow your body to breathe (as it's been doing all day and all night without any help from you)? Allow your attention just to rest lightly and feel the breath.

If your mind is trying to control your breathing, just notice this and return your attention – as many times as necessary – to the sensations of your breath moving in and out in your body.

Exercise: Mindfulness of Breathing

1 Choose to sit in the most comfortable position for your body, in this moment.

2 Tune into the sensations that tell you that your body is sitting in this place (see previous page).

3 Now you are exploring the experience in your body of breathing. Notice the movement as you breathe in and breathe out. Where do you feel your breath most strongly – at the tip of your nose, in your chest, in your ribcage, or maybe in your abdomen or belly?

4 With no need to change the flow of your breath in any way, just explore the feeling of the breath (see picture) and the texture, shape, pattern and rhythm of your breaths. Are they: Slow? Fast? Smooth? Shallow? Deep?

5 Follow each breath as it moves in, pauses, and then begins to travel back out again, pausing briefly before the next in-breath. Maybe imagine a beach – the breath is like the sea rolling up the sand as the waves move in and then retreat ready for the next wave to roll in.

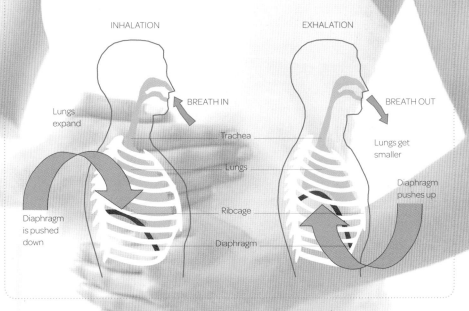

INHALATION

BREATH IN

Lungs expand

Trachea

Lungs

Ribcage

Diaphragm

Diaphragm is pushed down

EXHALATION

BREATH OUT

Lungs get smaller

Diaphragm pushes up

Mindfulness of the Body

There are many different ways that we can practise mindfulness. Sometimes we do a guided meditation practice, listening to a mindfulness teacher in a class or using a CD. The guidance structures the practice, anchoring our focus and helping us to notice when our mind wanders away. Sometimes practice is done in silence, following a chosen format without guidance. These practices are a pause in everyday life and a choice to spend a period of time specifically practising mindfulness meditation. Our focus is often our internal experience although it may also be what we see or hear. This kind of meditation is often called "formal practice".

Another kind of practice, which we explored in the last chapter, is when we bring mindful awareness to the activities of our day, and this is often called "informal practice". In informal practice our focus may be our internal experience, but it is more likely to be a mixture of our thoughts, emotions and body, and our experience of our surroundings.

Both of these types of meditation practice help us to develop our sensitivity to noticing our experience and our ability to choose where we focus our attention.

In both formal and informal practice we are exploring the whole package of our experience, sensations, emotions and thoughts, and also our relationship with this experience. We can begin to see how it all interconnects. We start to see the rich, complex texture of our experience and the moment-by-moment living of our life.

In practising mindfulness we are learning about ourselves, seeing our experience as clearly as we can, and watching our habits and the patterns of how we act and react to ourselves and our situations.

Exercise: Awareness of Body Sensations

This practice encourages a broad beam of focus: noticing the whole body, the surface it's lying or sitting on, and also the area around your body. You are opening your awareness to a whole range of sensations. You can explore this practice either sitting or lying down – whichever is better for you *in this moment.*

1 If you are choosing to lie down, find a position that will allow your body to be comfortable, and as supported as it can be by the floor/mat/rug/bed. Alternatively, you may prefer to do this practice sitting down (see below for a seated option). Although you are not *trying* to become relaxed as such, it is nevertheless helpful to let the body be at ease as you explore the different sensations.

2 If it feels comfortable, lie with your legs uncrossed and allow your feet to fall apart from one another. This position will allow your muscles to be at rest – they do not need to be actively working in order to hold your body in this position. If you have problems with your lower back, you may find it more comfortable to lie with your knees slightly bent and your feet flat on the floor (perhaps with a cushion tucked underneath to support them).

3 Allow your arms to rest by your sides with the palms facing upward (if that's comfortable).

4 Bring your attention now to the whole of your body as you lie here. What sensations do you notice?

THE SEATED VERSION

If you choose to sit to explore the sensations in your body, it's important to use a straight-backed chair rather than an armchair, and to sit with your feet fully in contact with the floor. A straight-backed chair will allow your body to be upright and tall. If it is OK for your body, it can also be helpful to sit away from the back of the chair so that your back is supporting itself. This allows for the natural curvature of the spine, which in turn helps the back, neck and head to be balanced. The invitations to notice sensations are just the same as those in the lying down position above.

Exercise: The Body Scan

You can also investigate the sensations in your body by zooming in your focus of attention to specific areas, slowly and a little at a time. You are inviting the mind to settle and rest gently – as much as it will – in the particular part of the body that you are choosing to explore, and to simply receive whatever sensations are there.

1 Allow your attention "beam" to explore one area of your body, then let it go from your mind's eye.

2 Now place attention on the next part for a few moments to explore experiences appearing here.

3 Release that area from your focus and move the focus again, continuing to choose whichever part of the body you wish to investigate.

Can you be precise about this experience?

- Do the sensations stay the same?
- Are the sensations in the form of colours or maybe sounds? Do you feel them in your body?
- Do you feel the pressure of your body on the floor? If so, where?
- Do you feel lightness or heaviness?
- Can you feel the contact of your clothes or air on your skin?
- Is there any tingling or pulsing?
- Do you notice tightness or looseness in your muscles?
- Do you feel numbness or intensity?
- What thoughts appear? What does your mind have to say about all this?

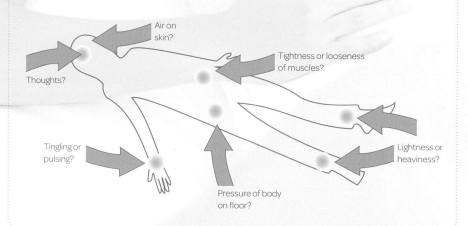

Air on skin?

Tightness or looseness of muscles?

Thoughts?

Tingling or pulsing?

Pressure of body on floor?

Lightness or heaviness?

Mind Wandering during Body Scans

The body can be a wonderful measure of how often and far the mind wanders! When we scan our bodies with a mindfulness teacher, a voice guides us. This reminds us to return our attention if it wanders away, and gives us some prompts as to what to "look" for as we investigate.

Even when we fully intend to pay attention to the whole body, we often find that parts of the body have "disappeared"! Sometimes we are aware that our mind has wandered, but the Body Scan can give us a clear sense of *how long* for. Sometimes we know exactly what we've been thinking about; at other times, not.

The exploration of the wandering mind is just as much part of the practice as being curious about body sensations. Are you able to bring friendliness to your wandering mind and be genuinely interested in its travels? As you practise, notice how many times you need to refocus your mind's attention on the body. Are you aware which area you were exploring in your body before the mind was diverted by a thought or perhaps a physical sensation elsewhere. Do you have a sense of how long your mind was away from this moment?

Sleepiness and the Body Scan

Our bodies are often chronically tired and will take any opportunity to catch up on some sleep, especially when we lie down. Approaching our sleepiness in mindfulness practice can be very interesting. We can discover many things:

- Sometimes we go out like a light. At other times we drift in and out of sleep.
- We are much more likely to fall asleep at certain times of the day than at others.
- We may be accepting of our sleepiness, or perhaps we are self-critical about it?
- Maybe we feel sleepy each time we scan a particular part of our body.
- Maybe we try to find ingenious ways to stay alert or choose to move our practice to a time when we generally feel less tired. Notice how these responses feel different to critical and forcing reactions to falling asleep.

Exploring the Body Moving

We have looked at how you can mindfully pay attention to your body when it is still, noticing your breath moving in and out. Paying attention to your body as it moves is another possibility. Our bodies spend a lot of time moving as we go about the daily business of our lives. But how often during the day do we really notice the sensations in our body? Here is a real opportunity to bring mindful attention right into your life, noticing how your body feels in motion.

Our physical sensations can give us very useful information about the state of our body and our emotions. If we learn to be receptive to these messages, it can help us to be in our lives more fully and make choices about how we act and behave.

- If we can feel our body rushing, we can *choose* to slow down.
- If we notice our jaw is very tight, we can realize that we are tense about something and perhaps *respond* to this.
- If we allow ourselves to *feel* ourselves in the process of moving somewhere, rather than being lost in thoughts about where we are going, we can actually be here in our life as it actually is.

Experiencing Daily Activities

As mindfulness is simply about paying attention in a friendly, interested way, we can bring this attitude to any activity in our lives. When we turn toward our experience, the experience may feel very different (as we saw with eating mindfully). We can wake up to details that we've missed for many years.

You may like to experiment with bringing mindful attention to other things that make up your everyday life, such as getting dressed, having a shower, feeding the dog or cat, gardening, washing up, driving the car or riding your bike.

Perhaps you can focus on all your senses as you carry out one of these activities, or maybe just pay attention to what you see, or hear or smell.

When we turn toward
our experience,
we can wake up to
details we've missed
for many years.

Exercise: Mindful Walking

Walking is something that we do naturally in all kinds of situations, but we rarely pay attention to putting one foot in front of the other unless it is painful to walk.

1 Begin by coming to stand. You might choose to do this in bare feet in order to increase your sensitivity to this exploration.

2 Notice the sensations of your feet in contact with the ground. Which parts of your feet are actually touching it? What do you feel? Are there more sensations in your toes or in your heels, at the sides or on the balls of your feet? Is your weight evenly distributed between your feet and through each foot, or do you perhaps feel more pressure in certain places in your feet? You could perhaps experiment by shifting your weight a little in different directions to feel the sensations alter as you move.

3 Expand your attention now to slowly scan your whole body, feeling all parts of it standing here, breathing.

4 When you are ready, bring the beam of awareness back – just to the area of the feet.

5 Now you're going to begin to move, so make the decision to shift your weight over onto one foot. Feel how the sensations shift as you do this. *Please note*: Walking slowly can be very challenging for our balance. If you know that your balance is somewhat unreliable then please walk where you can hold onto something safely, or alternatively you can choose to walk a little faster.

6 Slowly take a step forward now and tune in to the moment when your heel makes contact with the floor. Can you feel the pressure and contact of your heel against the floor?

7 Explore the sensations unfolding as the rest of your foot gradually makes contact with the floor.

8 Feel the weight fully on this foot as the other foot leaves the ground and swings through to take the next step.

9 Repeat this slowly, walking perhaps in a circle around the room or maybe in a straight line, pausing and turning when needed.

10 When your mind wanders or is caught by things it sees or hears, just notice this and gently but firmly bring your attention back to the sensations in your feet. You may need to invite your mind to resettle many times, and that's fine. (It is *returning our attention* to sensations as they are now that is mindfulness, waking up to this moment repeatedly. It is not about fixing or holding our focus in one place as the mind *will* wander – that's just what minds do!)

EXPAND THIS PRACTICE

- Connect your breath experience with your feet as they step. Breathe out as one foot steps forward, and in as the other moves through the air to take the next step. Allow your breath to time your steps.
- Experiment with changing the speed of walking, from walking very slowly to quickly.
- Focus your attention on more of your body as you walk, so that you are feeling other aspects of walking such as your arms swinging or the whole body moving.
- Pay attention to what you can see and hear around you.
- Perhaps try running mindfully!

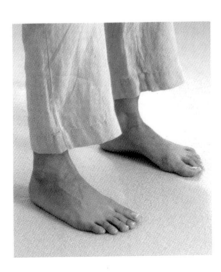 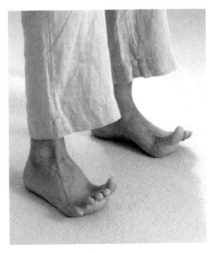

Mindful Movement

You can practise mindful movement by performing specific movements that wouldn't normally be part of your everyday life – creating postures and shapes which give you an opportunity to practise tuning in to your body's messages. There are no set ways of doing this and the choice you make will depend on your fitness levels, any limitations in your body just now due to illness or injury, and the amount of space available to you.

It is really important not to push yourself beyond what is wise for your body, in this moment. If you are not sure what your body is able to do without causing it difficulty or harm, please be sure to check with your family doctor or physiotherapist/physical therapist.

The aim of mindful movement is not to lose weight or to get fit; it is not about becoming stronger or more flexible; it is simply to notice sensations in the body as we move.

Investigating Limits and "Edges" in Mindful Movement

An interesting learning experience that can arise from this kind of mindful movement is finding, and becoming familiar with, our limits or "edges", and noticing how we deal with these when we encounter them. The place where our comfort begins to be challenged when we stretch or balance will manifest itself. This challenge may be the direct result of tightness in our muscles or restrictions in our joints. Alternatively, it may come from our thinking and emotions. These edges can be surprisingly variable, depending on many factors such as the time of day or our mood.

As you practise, you are invited to notice your limits and "edges".

- What happens when you breathe into these sensations?
- Do you find yourself habitually pushing through difficult experiences, or quickly pulling back to remove discomfort?
- Do you find that through effort and forcing yourself to carry on, you reduce or add to the strength of this edge?
- What happens to the experience of your limits if you criticize yourself?
- How do thoughts that dwell on times when your body worked better or was more flexible impact on the tightness of your body at this limit?
- What is the impact of creating ease and playfulness during these moments?
- What happens if you gently encourage yourself, and sensitively respond to what your body tells you?
- Can you respond with kindness and wisdom when your body and mind are at this edge and are reluctant to let go of the struggle here?

You can learn a lot about yourself by becoming better acquainted with the habits of your mind and body. Directly experiencing how you interact with and relate to difficulty will influence your sense of this edge, which has initially felt so fixed and unworkable.

With practice, you will feel how moments of stillness are really many dynamic micro-adjustments as you balance. You may discover that if you soften and ease yourself into stretches, you can stretch more deeply than if you try and push yourself to achieve.

The mindful exploration of the sensations that are here, right at this edge, and how you react and relate to these experiences, can offer you opportunities to practise and develop new ways of being with other "edges" in your life.

Now, if you choose to, you can try practising some mindful movement with the gentle exercises on the following pages.

Exercise: Standing and Sitting Movements

In choosing mindful movements it is important to not just work a few of your muscles, or only the muscles on one side, but rather the front and back, the right- and the left-hand side of your body. Choose combinations from the following:

ANYTIME STRETCH

Standing relaxed, raise your arms to shoulder height, taking care not to lift your shoulders. Turn your palms down. Draw your navel in to your spine and hold it there for the rest of the exercise. Draw your right arm into your back, moving it down and in simultaneously. Release and repeat on the other side, up to eight times each.

SIDE TWIST

1   Sit sideways on a chair with your feet flat on the floor. Cross your right arm in front of your waist and place your right hand on the chair back. Bring your left hand to the back of your head.

2   Breathe in and, as you breathe out, turn your head to the right. Lift your elbow toward the ceiling to gently stretch your left side, moving your right shoulder down toward the floor. Repeat five times on each side.

STANDING STRETCH

1 Stand with your feet hip width apart with the knees slightly bent and feet parallel.

2 Breathe in, raising your arms out to the sides. Breathe out, raising your arms until your hands meet above your head.

3 Continue to stretch upward, feeling the stretch all along the body. Gently breathe in and out, noticing any sensations.

4 Slowly, breathing out, allow the arms to come back down.

5 Close your eyes and focus attention on your breath, noticing any changes as the arms rest by your side.

6 Raise both arms up high, hands together, then bend to the right, with the hips going over to the left. Return to a central position and then bend over in the opposite direction.

7 Return to a central standing position. Observe the sensations in your body.

Three-Step Breathing Space

The Three-Step Breathing Space is distinguished by its hourglass "shape" – broad, narrow, broad. As you can see from the diagram opposite, the aim is to have an initial broad awareness of your experience, followed by a reducing or narrowing of the focus onto your breath, followed by an expansion of focus once more. The other helpful aspect of the Three-Step Breathing Space is that it can fit right into everyday life. It may *seem* like an easy version of the longer practices described so far, but it is actually quite challenging and immensely important. It invites us to:

- *Pause* and "change gear", right in the middle of the busy-ness of our lives.
- Stand steadily in our moment and just be.
- Be willing to really open to receive the detail of our experience, however it is.
- Resist the urge to *do* in this moment, or try to change and fix our experiences.
- Change our focus of attention over the three specific steps – from wide to narrow, and again to a wide focus.

You can introduce the Three-Step Breathing Space by choosing three times in your day to practise. It can be helpful to connect it to a routine activity, such as boiling the kettle or washing your hands. These activities can act as reminders and become natural pauses in the day for you to connect with your experience and move out of "autopilot".

The breathing space can be a helpful first step when things are stressful or challenging, by offering you space to decide an appropriate response to how things *actually are for you* in this moment. There is *no intention to change your experience* as you take a breathing space but it's a steady place to take a next step.

The Three Steps

1.

What's here? Receiving experience as it is ... Sensations in the body? Activity of the mind? Busy or calm? Certain thoughts/ preoccupations? Emotional tone?

2.

Focusing on just the sensations of the breath moving in and out of the body.

3.

Expanding the focus to experience the whole body in this place. Connection with the ground, the chair? Shape of the body? Posture? Expression? Space the body takes up? Space around the body in this place?

Part II

Mindfulness
with Life's Challenges

Mindfulness offers a response to a range of difficulties because the focus is on how we meet them rather than the difficulties themselves.

Working with Difficulty

In the second part of this book we are going to look at some of the many different contexts where mindfulness can be helpful. Often these situations are places in our lives where we meet our "edges" or are challenged. The problems inherent in each may look and feel very different from one another. However, mindfulness is able to offer a response to this range of difficulties because the focus is on how we meet them rather than on the difficulties themselves.

As we have been exploring together so far in this book, mindfulness offers us a way of seeing our experience clearly, as it is in this moment. This can really help us to connect to aspects of experience such as, perhaps, tasting delicious food, sharing a hug with our children or watching a beautiful sunset. We can actually feel, see and hear the park, the beach or the mountains as we walk, allowing us to appreciate and sense a connection with the world we live in. We are opening ourselves up to the experiences that already exist in our lives.

But how appropriate is this when the circumstances of our lives are maybe actively challenging, and not enjoyable or how we want them to be?

It is human nature to react strongly to experiences that are perceived as unpleasant. For example, when we feel discomfort or pain (either physical or emotional), we may well want things to be different from how they currently are. Of course, if it is easy to resolve the difficulties that occur in our lives, this is what we will do. It is natural to want to change, move away or escape from both the circumstances and the physical sensations or emotions that cause us to suffer. But with many challenging situations, it's not always that straightforward. Often there is no easy solution, and even when we have tried everything, the unwanted situation remains.

So how can mindfulness be relevant when we find ourselves "at the edge"? After all, it invites us to turn toward the challenging circumstances in our life and investigate them closely. Surely that would make things feel much worse? Surprisingly, we find that this is not the case.

It can be helpful here to make a comparison with the weather. The weather has many different "moods" and changes continually – in some parts of the world more than others! Some days the wind blows a gale, the rain lashes down and it's freezing cold, while other days are warm, sunny, still and calm. This is just how it is. Even though we may not like it sometimes, we do understand that this is how the weather behaves – we can't control it or even reliably predict it; we just have to adapt and respond to whatever conditions it brings.

You may find it interesting to ask yourself whether you see your life and your experience in this way. Are you as accepting of the fact that the circumstances of your life will vary? Is it equally OK that life will sometimes be stormy and challenging and at other times it will be calm and peaceful? Have you understood that whatever your current circumstances are, they *will* change and that nothing lasts forever?

Often we have a belief – or maybe just a hope – that our lives can and should be perpetually sunny and calm, without any difficult and stressful experiences to challenge us. If we believe this, then it follows that we might be trying to achieve this steady, pleasant state of affairs and therefore feel very frustrated, dissatisfied and disappointed if things do not turn out that way (remember we saw how the doing mode of mind can often encourage this view; see pages 36–45). It is normal to want to hold on to the lovely moments in life and to avoid, escape or fix the difficult ones. But although this is expected and understandable, all this effort may not be able to get us what we would really like. Unless we choose to move to a part of the world where we can guarantee different weather, mostly we just need to find appropriate ways to *adapt* to the weather we find in our lives.

Encountering Difficulty

The following examples present a difficulty or challenge you may encounter, such as chronic pain, worrying thoughts, acute illness, a challenging boss, a large fuel bill, an argumentative teenager, a traffic jam or a task at work that pushes you to your limits. These can be experiences that come from within you, or externally, from events or from people you meet or share your life with.

We sometimes demonstrate encountering such challenges in mindfulness classes because this helps us to connect with how it feels as we react to the various difficulties in our lives – it also helps us to see what impact our feelings and reaction have on both the difficulty and ourselves. We often refer to the Dancing with Difficulty exercise (see page 78), in which the energy of an opponent's attack is met and directed rather than blocked or overcome, as the "Aikido Exercise" since it is drawn from that martial art.

Mindfulness offers us a different way to respond as it can help us to develop skills in seeing all circumstances clearly and build our repertoire of responses. We can step out of habitual patterns of reacting and learn to respond wisely instead. We can be awake to our choices and feel how any action we take interplays with our difficulties. There is an active relationship between us and them. As you consider these, you may recognize ways in which you tend to deal with difficulty in your life. Is one way familiar, or are there perhaps several?

SHOCK

You may not know how to respond in this moment. The difficulty may knock you off balance, or you may feel like it has knocked you flat. For example:

- An unexpectedly big utilities bill arrives through the door.
- A friend tells you they have been diagnosed with cancer.

AVOIDANCE

You are trying to distance yourself from something and the feelings it stirs up in you. However, in spite of your efforts to avoid it, you realize that this doesn't make it go away. For example:

- You have a bad experience with an argumentative person while travelling home on the bus one evening, so you decide to avoid all bus travel from now on. But you still have to get home from work somehow.
- You are sometimes required to give presentations at work, and while you've been told that the presentations you have given thus far are fine, you are so anxious about speaking in public, that you decide to change your job. But other jobs may also need you to make presentations.

BURYING YOUR HEAD IN THE SAND

You want to retreat from a difficulty and hope that, if you curl up and hide, it will have gone away by the time you emerge. But this difficulty is going nowhere and is still there when you emerge again. For example:

- You have been having problems in your relationship and have dealt with it by pretending it will pass and you don't need to do anything.
- Your teenage son or daughter is staying out really late with friends you don't approve of, but you persuade yourself that it's just a phase that will pass.

DOING BATTLE

You meet a difficulty head-on, and try your best to beat it and make it go away. But you find that the difficulty just pushes back at you, and as you continue to do battle you get more and more tired. For example:

- You have been working really hard and are tired and stressed, but decide that if you just work that little bit more, you will get it all done and things will be OK.
- You are worried that you may have a serious health problem, and buy all the available remedies to make yourself better. You are not going to let it beat you.

Exercise: Dancing with Difficulty

Like an Aikido fighter facing an adversary, through mindfulness you can experience meeting the difficulty in your life.

1 As you approach your "adversary" at close quarters, you are balanced and stable, firmly connected to the ground.

2 Seeing and feeling your difficulty in detail, you notice its character and patterns.

3 Even if it is really powerful, if you move in close you can redirect or deflect its energy or force.

4 Now the energy is deflected, it is possible to move so that you and your "adversary" are side by side. Neither of you is leaning on the other.

5 Now it is possible to steer the force, even if it remains powerful, choosing the direction you move in.

6 And this can become a dance like a tango rather than a battle.

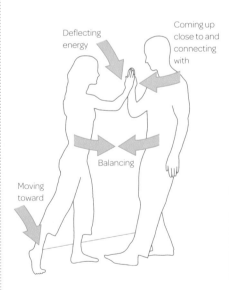

Deflecting energy

Coming up close to and connecting with

Balancing

Moving toward

Alison had experienced constant and uncontrollable back pain for years following a car crash. The pain affected many aspects of her life, including sleep, and she was always tired. She was irritable and in a low mood for much of the time. She felt really angry about the person who had caused the crash. Her mind kept replaying the crash and her previously active life, but this led to feelings of fury and hopelessness. For a while she avoided her pain through drugs and alcohol.

When Alison began to practise mindfulness, at first she was sceptical, but at the same time she needed it to be "the answer". As her mindfulness practice developed, and she learned to see how things were with curiosity and warmth toward herself, she noticed that she felt less afraid and less tense. It was possible to move toward the experiences she was having with some degree of ease and gentleness both to herself and her pain. She had thought that she knew her back pain inside and out, but with mindful awareness she saw the detail of it more clearly. She saw its patterns and could recognize the interactive nature of her physical, emotional and thinking processes. She saw how her anger tightened her body, adding to the pain, and how the thoughts that replayed in her mind significantly lowered her mood. She also noticed, with surprise, that there were times in her day when she wasn't in pain, and even when she was this didn't necessarily stop her enjoying things in her life.

Of course, specific life circumstances influence our experience. In the first half of the book we have noticed how our own perception, the meaning of this situation to us, and our response, can be important. Mindfulness can help us develop flexibility and resilience through simply being present with our experience, seeing all aspects of internal and external experience clearly, and being creative in how we respond or "dance" with it, even if it is challenging. Watching skilled surfers on a big wave, we see the interplay of them and that particular wave. Their balance and sensitivity to the wave's energy and unfolding nature, and to their own posture on the board, allow a dynamic relationship between the surfers and the wave. Mindfulness practice can allow us to learn to "surf the waves of our lives".

04.

Mindfulness
and Depression

By Sarah Silverton

Depression is very common: it affects one in four people at some point in their lives.

Symptoms of Depression

Depression is a common condition affecting one in four people at some point in their lives. According to the World Health Organization (WHO), there are about 121 million people with depression worldwide. People often don't realize how common it is because sufferers generally don't talk about this experience easily – even with family and close friends – and it may not be obvious to others.

People use the term "depression" in daily life to describe a range of emotions such as sadness, disappointment and maybe even frustration or boredom. Used in this way it is usually describing emotions that all of us can expect to feel as life offers challenges and unexpected twists and turns. Depression as a *condition*, however, is a very different experience from the sadness that most people recognize. It is also important to underline that depression often goes hand-in-hand with anxiety.

THE CYCLE OF DEPRESSION

Our body, emotions, thoughts and behaviour all *interact* when we are depressed and as we react to this painful experience. Although everyone's experience of depression will be a unique combination, opposite are some symptoms commonly described by people who experience depression. Doctors will diagnose depression when five or more of these are experienced continuously over a period of at least two weeks.

Pessimistic or self-blaming thoughts, which are common in depression, can trigger low mood and directly affect our body sensations. Low mood in turn increases the likelihood of negative thoughts. The state of our body can also have a direct impact on our emotions. Being tired, for example, can make us feel down, and even lowering our gaze and sitting with our posture slumped and "closed" for a period of time can lower our mood and trigger depressed thinking.

Body

- Fatigue
- Feeling physically slowed down
- Sleep disturbances – such as difficulty sleeping, early morning waking or sleeping much more than usual
- Appetite disturbance – such as loss of appetite or comfort eating
- Weight gain or loss
- Crying/tearfulness
- Anxiety

Emotions

- Sadness
- Lethargy
- Loss of interest in things that normally are enjoyable
- Irritation
- Anger
- Feeling numb/disconnected from emotions
- Guilt
- Shame

Thoughts

- Self-critical • Pessimistic
- Discouraging • Feeling guilty about something inappropriately
- Questioning/doubting self-worth
- Believing that things are wrong or not quite right as they are (in oneself or in one's life)
- Thoughts about death
- Rumination – thoughts may go round and round one's head and be difficult to "switch off"
- Difficulty concentrating or thinking clearly

Behaviour

- Withdrawal from normal activities
- Social isolation/avoiding social contact
- Engaging in activities that act as a distraction from feelings or block out thoughts – such as over-working, or using drugs or alcohol
- Altered eating patterns – either more or less than usual
- Taking to one's bed
- Altered sleep patterns – either more or less sleep than usual
- Being argumentative

Causes of Depression

Depression can be caused by a combination of factors. Biochemical imbalance is thought to be one cause and is more obvious in some kinds of depression, such as postnatal depression. Antidepressant medication aims to redress biochemical imbalance.

Depression can also be triggered by life events. These may include difficult relationships with parents or others who cared for us when we were young, or adversity, trauma or loss at any time in our lives.

There is also growing evidence that the more episodes of depression someone has had, the more readily depression will return. After two episodes the triggers for it become sensitized. John Teasdale (see pages 14–17) highlights how sensitive this reaction may become over time, where even normal experiences such as waking up feeling tired one morning, or sadness that is completely understandable, can start a process where depression can be re-established. If we don't notice this pattern, our depressive experience can develop, unfold and become established without us realizing. Many people have no idea why an episode of depression began and, understandably, find this very frightening.

Patterns of Reaction

While you read this chapter you might notice altered sensations in your body or changes in your mood. Just reading certain words may remind us of times when we were depressed and open us to mood and body shifts that relate to these. The trigger can be something that happens in our life or an experience in our body or mind. This experience starts a physical and mental "flow" or chain of events. Depending on the nature of these, we may actually *intensify* the initial experience (see page 104 for how our view of past experience may colour the present).

How Assumptions Create Meaning

You are expecting a friend to call but she doesn't ...

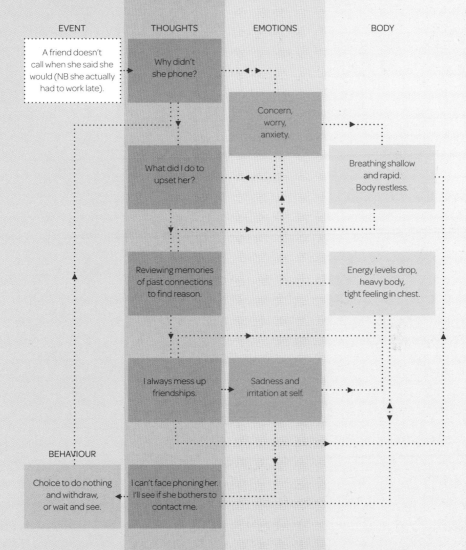

EVENT THOUGHTS EMOTIONS BODY

A friend doesn't call when she said she would (NB she actually had to work late).

Why didn't she phone?

Concern, worry, anxiety.

Breathing shallow and rapid. Body restless.

What did I do to upset her?

Reviewing memories of past connections to find reason.

Energy levels drop, heavy body, tight feeling in chest.

I always mess up friendships.

Sadness and irritation at self.

BEHAVIOUR

Choice to do nothing and withdraw, or wait and see.

I can't face phoning her. I'll see if she bothers to contact me.

This chain of thoughts and emotions does not match the circumstances – that the friend had to work late.

How We View Experiences

We receive and make sense of the huge volume of our experiences constantly. In doing so we don't take in all the information equally but rather select information based on the way that we tend to see the world. We pick up on some things and miss others. It's as if we are wearing lenses that filter our experience.

Reports given by witnesses to a crime vary hugely – even fundamental details may have been perceived in a radically different way by people who saw the same event. When we look at ourselves in a mirror we often home in on our least favourite feature, not noticing the qualities we like!

The Creative Mind Filling in the Gaps

We receive information about our experiences through this perceptive lens, and then this information is also *interpreted* so that we can make sense of it. Our mind needs to *know*. This is a normal human process that affects us all, but it has particular significance for those who get depressed. If we don't know all the facts, our mind finds it very hard to acknowledge what it doesn't know and will busily try to fill in the gaps. Optical illusions are a good way of demonstrating how the mind looks for meaning.

Our mind fills in the gaps of our understanding, drawing on our past experience and our core beliefs about ourselves and our lives. Because the information is so familiar, it is likely that the story that our mind creates will be very credible to us: it will make sense and seem to fit the information we have. We are then much less likely to question our assumptions and can find ourselves acting on them as if they are proven, indisputable facts. If you are depressed, the assumptions you make may be quite different to those of someone who is well and positive.

Susie on the bus

Read these sentences one at a time and notice the image that comes to mind *after each sentence* of this scenario:

....

1.

Susie is travelling on a bus on a route that she often travels.

....

2.

She has a favourite teddy sitting on her lap and she feels very happy.

....

3.

She can't wait to see her granddaughter as it has been a long time.

....

4.

Her recent trip sailing solo around the world took her away from her family for many months.

....

What did you notice? Did your mind conjure up pictures and ideas of who Susie is? Did this picture change as you gathered more information about her?

Dealing with Depression

The experience of depression is difficult and deeply unpleasant. Naturally, we don't want to feel like this and will avoid or try to fix this experience if at all possible. Many people's strategies intend to numb or avoid the pain of depression.

These coping strategies may work well for short periods. Retreating to bed can seem like a reasonable solution to the experience of painful and believable thoughts, a tired body, and feeling vulnerable and unsociable. Sleeping can provide some respite from this pain. But on waking, things are still the same and lying in bed just gives uninterrupted time to think frightening or upsetting thoughts. We may also have cut ourselves off from family and friends, who perhaps could help us find a new perspective or support us through this painful experience.

A Radically Different Approach

As we have seen in the previous pages, while our mind tries to help by making sense of our experience, we can unwittingly add to the distress we feel by trying to think our experience through. This process is sometimes called *rumination*. How we see and make sense of experience and the subsequent unfolding of thoughts, emotions and sensations in our body can happen very quickly and, for the most part, automatically. We may find ourselves stuck in a mental rut, thinking the usual thoughts, feeling the emotions connected with these and behaving in our habitual ways without choosing to do so.

On the other hand, as we explored in Part I of this book, noticing our experience though mindfulness practice, standing back a little and making some space for it to be as it is in this moment – even when it is a very difficult experience – can fundamentally change the way we perceive it.

The invitation of mindfulness to move closer and see and feel the detail of experience can feel counter-intuitive but actually makes a lot of sense. Imagine you are driving in winter and find yourself on an icy road – what would you do?

• Ignore the information that the road is icy and travel at the same speed as before, regardless?
• Stop the car and not go any further because of what might happen?
• Speed up to get past this dangerous situation as fast as possible?

Alternatively, you might:

• Slow down and assess the details of the situation that you find yourself in.
• Check the road as far as is visible to see if there are many patches of ice or just this one.
• Check the gradient of the road further on.
• Look at whether the road is wide or narrow, and if there are ditches or wide verges at the sides.
• Judge the capability of your vehicle to tackle these conditions on the road.
• Acknowledge your own skills and experience of driving in these conditions.

With this information you could choose an appropriate course of action. Maybe it is safe to continue driving if this is just one isolated puddle that has iced over; or you may need to change gear and slow down; maybe you could fit ice chains to the tyres; or perhaps you should turn around and continue by another route. *None of these options requires the road to change.*

Mindfulness allows us to be with the painful experience of being depressed in a similar way: seeing our internal and external environments clearly and quickly, even if they feel threatening and dangerous places to be. This, in turn, offers us options for how best to respond.

The Mindful Response

As we explored earlier, our thoughts, emotions, body and behaviour all interrelate. As we learn to respond to our experience mindfully, it is important to remember this. Focusing our response on our body will also influence our mood, and responding to our thoughts will affect our body and emotions, too.

Maybe when your thoughts are particularly powerful, the wisest path is to choose a response that focuses on the tightness that is also appearing in your body. Or if your body is really heavy and tired, kindness and encouraging thoughts may be a more accessible response than a movement practice.

Step Back or "De-centre"

The moment we pause and have a look at how things actually are for us just now, we have taken a step out of the middle of the dense "fog" of depression. We have found a different place that will give us a different perspective on our experience. The ability to pause, de-centre and explore what's here can allow us to find that the fog *isn't all there is* and *it doesn't go on for ever*.

Bringing Gentle Curiosity to What's Here

Developing curiosity about our experience is another important shift. Curiosity involves *approaching* our difficult experience rather than the natural reaction (to turn away from it or try to make it go away). As we approach and are curious about difficult experience, we are more creative in our responses. We can distinguish our thoughts, emotions and body sensations and see their interactions. As our experience of mindfully being with difficulty grows, we become much less afraid of feeling this way and know that it is safe to explore these experiences.

Seeing Thoughts as Mental Events

Thoughts, especially those that come with strong and painful emotions, are probably the most difficult experiences to stay present with when we practise mindfulness. They often deliver powerful propaganda that pulls us into their stories. It can take some practice to step back from the content and characters in your thoughts to see them clearly. It can be useful to consider the following:

- What are your thoughts saying? Are they about the past (reflections, memories, reviewing events), the future (anticipating, planning, worrying), or about now (commentary, judgement)?
- Do you recognize familiar thoughts?
- If you compare these thoughts to passing clouds, are they light and wispy or dark and heavy? Do they feel like they take up the whole sky?
- What is the speed or energy of the flow of thoughts? Are there lots of thoughts appearing or just a few powerful ones going round and round in your mind?
- Are these the kind of thoughts that tend to come when you are low in mood? Like a high fever accompanying influenza, maybe these thoughts can be seen as just a symptom with no need to pay them much attention or believe what they have to say?
- Notice the flavour and "distortions" of your thoughts. Are they over-generalizing or crystal-ball gazing and predicting the future? Perhaps there are lots of "should", "must" or "ought to" thoughts appearing?
- Become friendly with these thoughts and with yourself as you experience them. Maybe you might even welcome your thoughts as well-known visitors?
- Allow your thoughts to run without blocking them or having to challenge them, but without giving them much credence either.

If you imagine thoughts as trains, it can feel like we get on every train that passes, even if we don't want its destination! Our mind gets caught up with every idea, ending up in distant places apparently unconnected to our starting point.

Mindfulness allows us to *decide* whether to step on a thought train or not and, if we find ourselves inadvertently aboard, allows us to choose to get off at the next stop rather than ride all the way to the end of the line.

This approach to depressive thoughts is somewhat different from other therapeutic approaches. Some approaches focus on analyzing the thoughts that arise to see why they are here and to discover their roots in our history. Other approaches invite us to, albeit gently, challenge our thoughts and find alternative thoughts that are more accurate and appropriate to current circumstances.

Mindfulness doesn't require us to "work" with our thoughts but rather invites us to develop a steady place from which to see them clearly. Making room for them in our experience, paradoxically, seems to give them much less strength.

Changing the Focus of Attention

We learn through practising mindfulness that we can choose our focus of attention and that even if our mind is still pulled to difficult places, we can refocus and place our attention where we want to. We can find alternative foci that allow us to feel steadier. We can bring our focus to:

- The *sensations of movement in our body* as we breathe. Our breath can act as an anchor to settle us here when our emotional weather is stormy.
- We can *hear* the sounds around us, focusing on the detail of these and also connecting to a broader picture of being in this moment.
- We can *see* details of what is here around us.

Mindfulness allows the *beam of our attention* to be filled with other experiences of our moment. Our experience is like a tapestry of many different threads, some of which are dark. When things are painful we may focus solely on what is sombre and lose sight of other experiences that are also here. However, the tapestry will always have other colours and textures of thread available to see and feel.

Opening our awareness to include the broad range of our experiences is very different to the defensive strategy of "walling off" the painful ones (by avoiding them or pushing them away). As we practise mindfulness we're allowing difficult experiences to be here, but – if we choose – in the background as part of the picture, rather than in the spotlight.

In mindfulness classes we invite people to keep a diary for a week, recording pleasant experiences (they don't need to be big) in their lives – you may like to try this yourself. Many people are happily surprised by how many pleasant experiences are already in their lives. They had just missed seeing them as they focused on their, supposedly more important, problematic experiences.

Being in This Moment

Mindful awareness of our experience *now*, rather than in the past or future, can offer a significant step toward allowing us a new perspective.

Hazel was waking early and finding her mind was busy and worried. She was also having worrying thoughts about what this sleep disturbance meant. Was she getting depressed again? These thoughts brought vivid and upsetting memories.

By bringing just her present moment's experience into focus, she saw that although she was awake early, she didn't feel tired and had had sufficient sleep. She noticed the speed and tone of her thoughts and recognized some familiar ones showing up. Rather than paying these thoughts too much attention, she decided to focus on the sensations in her body as they were in that moment. She made herself comfortable in bed and moved her mind slowly and gently through her body. She found that there were many experiences here that told her that things were fine in *this* moment. For example, she was warm and comfortable. Exploring her physical experience meant that her busy mind had something else to become involved with, in this moment.

Mindfulness allows us to see our internal and external environments clearly. This helps show us how best to respond.

Responding and Taking Care of Yourself

When we become aware of our habitual patterns and see that we are feeling low or vulnerable, this also allows us to choose ways to look after ourselves while – and because – we are feeling this way. We can learn to meet experience with a wise, friendly and flexible response. The following actions might be helpful:

- *Listening to music, dancing, having a warm bath, eating well, drinking a cup of tea or walking* can make you feel you have met your body or mind's needs.
- *Spending time with a good friend or pet, watching a sunset or receiving a hug* may help you feel less alone and part of something bigger than yourself.
- *Paying a bill, cleaning the car, deleting old emails or spring cleaning* can give you a sense of achievement or control in your life:
- *Drawing, writing poetry, dancing, tapestry,* or *gardening* are creativity and pleasurable ways to spend your time.
- *Tasting your food, feeling the warm water and smelling the gel as you shower, seeing the faces of your family as you eat together, washing the dishes, and driving your car* are some of the ways you can bring mindful awareness to everyday activities.

These are just a few possibilities of how you can choose to take care of yourself. It is important that whatever you choose is a response to what you are feeling in that moment, and that you do it as an *experiment* and with *mindful awareness*. You are engaging your curious "being" mind mode, rather than the mind that wants or needs things to be different. Even very small steps can make a big difference.

Movement Practice

When we are depressed, we often feel lethargic – our impulse is to retreat, curl up and stop. However, there is clear evidence that changing our posture to sit upright and tall, with the chest area open, shoulders back, our gaze raised and the chin lifted a little, will lift our mood. Smiling can also help, even if we don't feel happy.

Moving when we feel tired or low can feel counter-intuitive (it may even seem impossible). But movement or physical exercise can have a positive impact on our mood and energy levels. Energy can feel like it's a precious and limited resource that needs to be conserved. It may seem logical to wait until we feel our energy levels rise *before* we use our energy reserves. Surprisingly, this isn't the case.

A brisk walk, stretching or swimming regularly can really make a difference to body and mood. When our thoughts are pessimistic, powerful and convincing, approaching things from the different angle of our body may feel like a more possible response than directly responding to our thoughts.

Our energy, when we are depressed, is more like a spring than a pond. If we unblock the source of the spring through doing even very gentle and mindful movement then the energy can begin to flow again.

Kindness and Depression

The experience of depression is indeed painful and has many different facets. If a friend were feeling this way we would want to offer them support and kindness. Actually we find that many people who become depressed can find kindness very difficult to offer themselves or receive from other people. Kindness or compliments may be discounted as insincere or undeserved (or perhaps just not felt at all).

Initially, it may only be possible to notice the critical and unkind things we are saying and doing to ourselves. But maybe it is possible to choose to respond – even in a small way – with kindness and supportiveness toward ourselves *because* this is how we are thinking and feeling? Acknowledging that we're hurting may be a first and important step in being friendly to ourselves.

In Mindfulness-Based Cognitive Therapy (MBCT) classes (see pages 14–17) participants see others in the group being self-critical or unkind to themselves and realize that what this person is saying to him- or herself is untrue. This can be a helpful place to wonder: "When I am critical of myself, perhaps that is also unfair and untrue?" (For more on MBCT see page 178.)

05.

Mindfulness
for Stress
and Anxiety

By Vanessa Hope

Mindfulness invites us to turn toward our experiences because our attempts to change, fix or run away from them have not worked for us and our stress is still here.

How to Deal with Stress and Anxiety

Mindfulness training has been helping people with many kinds of stress for over 35 years. In fact, when Jon Kabat-Zinn (see pages 13–14) started teaching mindfulness in the 1970s, he called the course he offered "The Mindfulness-Based Stress Reduction Programme".

Since then life seems to have become increasingly stressful for all of us. Stress appears everywhere: at work, at home, in our relationships, in our finances, and along with stress come worrying thoughts that can create fear or anxiety that will impact on our bodies and emotions.

Why is mindfulness so helpful for reducing stress? As we have already seen throughout the book, mindfulness invites us to deal with difficulty in our lives in a radically different way. Mindfulness is not about trying to fix the causes of stress or get rid of difficulties (in fact, many of these are inescapably woven into the very fabric of our lives). Mindfulness training asks us instead to turn closely toward and investigate our difficulties, because this is our experience at this moment.

It is only when you look closely and understand what is really going on in your life that you can begin to make wise choices about actions you can take. Mindfulness invites you, as a first step, to explore and acknowledge your problems as they are for you in the present moment, and to give them your full attention.

Seeing Your Stress

Perhaps ask yourself this question: "What are the stresses in my life at the moment?" Reflect for a moment on them (maybe you could write them down). Are they to do with money? With work? With family?

Ask yourself: "How do I *react* when I am stressed about these problems?" The first thing that comes to mind may be the *consequence or result* of feeling stressed, such as shouting at someone. Perhaps write down what happens to your body and your mood. What thoughts come into your mind? What do you do?

You may notice here that we are teasing out the different strands of our experience. If we had a very tangled ball of wool or string, it would probably get into even more of a tangle if we tried to unknot it by pulling at a loose end. If, however, we gently tease apart the strands, then the knot will loosen and ease.

We tend to label what is happening as stress and then to see it as something solid and unmanageable. But if we investigate what *actually* happens, we begin to notice that our stress is made up of many things – and as we pause and see, the space which this creates offers us more possibility of working with our stress.

The Nature of Stress

Stress is the natural reaction of our body to a perceived threat. In times of emergency our basic instinct is to ensure our survival. In primitive times threats needed fast physical reactions. With your life threatened by a wild animal, your options were to attack, run away fast or stay very still. Our bodies react automatically and immediately to help us to do this. This happens with the help of the sympathetic nervous system, which releases the hormones adrenalin and cortisol to prepare us for action.

But, importantly, our body will react in the same ancient and programmed way whether the threat is external (like a car swerving toward us) or internal (such as worrying thoughts about asking our neighbours to make less noise and the possible consequences of this).

Physical Reactions

Opposite you can see some of the ways you might experience the stress reaction in your body. Perhaps you can begin to see how natural and instinctive those stress reactions you wrote down are (see page 100)?

In more primitive times, after we had responded to a threat by either attacking or running away, the adrenalin and cortisol would have been used up. This would have then triggered the parasympathetic nervous system, which releases different hormones – oxytocin and vasopressin – to calm our minds and bodies and bring us back into balance.

Of course, some stress in our lives is positive, such as the stress that can arise when we are promoted or when we get married – and boredom can also be very stressful.

In modern life stressors may not be physical threats but often arise from our thoughts, so they may be imagined rather than actual circumstances. The result of this is that we usually do not have the chance to react physically through fight, flight or freeze.

This means that we do not use up the stress hormones in our bodies. They continue to circulate, keeping us on high alert, and the calming parasympathetic nervous system is not activated. This leads to constant and sometimes chronic hyper-arousal of the sympathetic nervous system, which can in turn lead to problems for us such as: fatigue or tiredness, sleep disruption, headaches, backaches, high blood-pressure, anxiety or panic attacks. If this goes on for long enough, it may cause chronic physical and mental health problems such as: ulcers, heart problems, digestive problems and depression.

Inner and outer stresses can feed each other in a vicious circle. For example, if you cannot sleep, you become tired and run down. But worrying about the consequences of not sleeping may make sleep even less possible.

The Stress Reaction

A stressful event triggers the release of hormones such as adrenalin and cortisol. These in turn bring about changes in the body.

Getting sweaty makes you slippery and therefore more difficult to catch!

Your brain is on high alert, constantly scanning for further threats. Your mind is making rapid comparisons with similar previous experiences.

Muscle tension or tightness in the throat, neck, jaw and upper back.

Shoulders raised (and legs braced) so that you are ready to run or fight.

Raised heart rate and blood-pressure takes blood to your muscles.

Churning or "butterflies" in the stomach as blood is taken away from your digestive system to power your muscles. The urge to empty your bladder or bowels as this will make you lighter and therefore able to run faster.

The more stressed you get, the more anxious and restless your body feels, and this makes it hard to slow down and rest. To avoid feeling so anxious you may take care to avoid situations that could cause anxiety.

Worrying thoughts can be a significant form of stress in our lives. We may even become habitual worriers. Every little thing causes concern and we can worry about what *might* happen. This takes a lot of energy and may keep us almost permanently in fight-or-flight mode.

- Can you recognize familiar ways in which you deal with stress?
- Can you see fight, flight and freeze in your own reactions to stresses?
- Do you use all of them or just one?
- What do these reactions feel like?
- How effective are your responses in dealing with your stress?

Avoidance as a Coping Strategy

Avoidance is the equivalent of *flight* and deserves special note because it is one of the most common strategies for managing fear and stress in the modern world.

It is understandable that we avoid stressful circumstances where possible – for example, moving away from a snarling dog. This strategy may well be appropriate if the stress is external and is actually a threat to us in this moment.

Things become more complicated for us when we try to avoid stress that arises from within us – perhaps troubling memories and worries, or bodily sensations such as palpitations or tight muscles. We can also become afraid of our own fear. We can find ourselves generalizing, so that having been afraid on one occasion means that we believe, or become afraid that, this fearful reaction will now *always* happen.

We can be really creative in our attempts at avoidance! Distractions come in many different guises, including ways to *numb* the difficult sensations (alcohol or drugs often serve this purpose). Watching TV can stop us focusing on our work worries. Keeping really busy can also keep thoughts at bay and feel helpful if we're already feeling agitated or restless.

Avoiding certain activities that cause you to feel afraid (such as flying in an aeroplane) may not have a big impact on your daily life, but if you needed to avoid all public transport because you became anxious on a bus one day, this may be much more disruptive. If you avoid things because they *might* make you feel anxious, your life can be very restricted. Your horizons can become narrower and narrower in your attempts not to feel fear or its effects. As you avoid things, you are doing nothing to see the whole picture as it actually is now, or to develop your understanding of the roots of your fear and deal appropriately with it.

It becomes obvious that our inbuilt ways of dealing with stress, as natural as they are to us as human beings, frequently don't fit well in our modern world. They may even add to the level of stress we feel, even though we use them with the idea of relieving our stress and feeling better. In our attempts to resolve matters we may actually be "throwing logs on the fire" of our stress and anxiety.

Stress is a reaction to a perceived threat. It is not only the situation, but how we view it and our attitude to it, that cause us stress.

Responding to Stress

We have been looking at the ways in which we may react naturally (but unhelpfully) in stressful situations. But you can probably think of other ways in which you already instinctively help yourself when you get stressed.

So now try asking yourself another question: "What are my constructive responses to stress? What helpful strategies do I have?" Perhaps you use some of the following: taking some exercise, such as going for a run, having a swim, playing football, dancing; relaxing by having a warm bath, a massage, doing some stretches or yoga; expressing how you feel through music, art, dance, poetry or creating a garden; calling a friend to talk through a stressful situation in your life. But even if we have helpful strategies, the unhelpful ones may still be the first to appear and have a strong pull.

The Mindful Response to Stress

Mindfulness teaches us to move out of automatic pilot and into being mode, rather than reacting habitually. It is about choosing to shift mental gear to *be* fully here. In mindfulness we practise noticing when our minds move out of the present moment, and we learn to bring them back to where we actually are. When our attention wanders – as it surely will – we notice with *curiosity* where it has gone, and bring it back to our chosen, present-moment focus. We learn to do this with *patience and gentleness* because our wandering mind is part of being human.

You can begin to choose in each moment where to place your attention. This gives you the chance to turn toward and see how physical sensations, anxious feelings and frightening thoughts interact and unfold. You can choose to pause, step out of your reactivity and respond to this experience of stress. You are approaching rather than avoiding, as you gently bring curiosity to what's here. The Three-Step Breathing Space (see pages 70–71) can really help with this.

Stress Reaction versus Mindful Response

You see a dog in the street ...

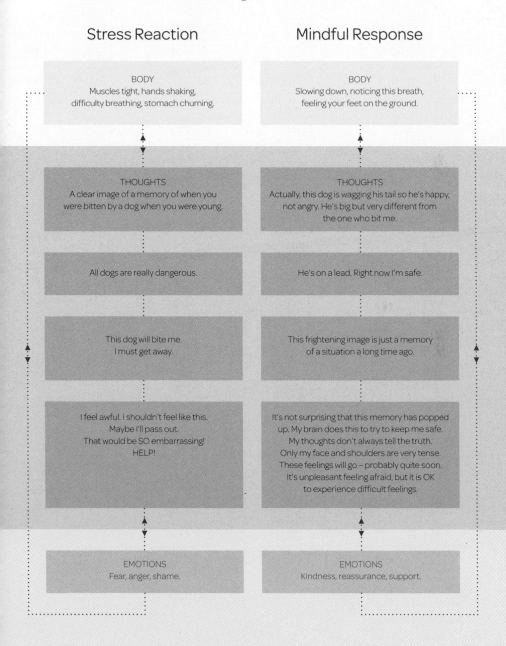

Stress Reaction	Mindful Response
BODY Muscles tight, hands shaking, difficulty breathing, stomach churning.	**BODY** Slowing down, noticing this breath, feeling your feet on the ground.
THOUGHTS A clear image of a memory of when you were bitten by a dog when you were young.	**THOUGHTS** Actually, this dog is wagging his tail so he's happy, not angry. He's big but very different from the one who bit me.
All dogs are really dangerous.	He's on a lead. Right now I'm safe.
This dog will bite me. I must get away.	This frightening image is just a memory of a situation a long time ago.
I feel awful. I shouldn't feel like this. Maybe I'll pass out. That would be SO embarrassing! HELP!	It's not surprising that this memory has popped up. My brain does this to try to keep me safe. My thoughts don't always tell the truth. Only my face and shoulders are very tense. These feelings will go – probably quite soon. It's unpleasant feeling afraid, but it is OK to experience difficult feelings.
EMOTIONS Fear, anger, shame.	**EMOTIONS** Kindness, reassurance, support.

Being in Your Body

Mindfulness practice emphasizes getting in touch with our bodies. Many of us think about our experience, paying little attention to what our bodies tell us. Society and education also encourage this cognitive processing. Our bodies are wonderful instruments; they graphically illustrate how and where we are feeling our stress and this gives us the opportunity to learn to respond wisely.

If you notice that your jaw is tight, your shoulders are hunched up or your hands are clenched, it alerts you to the fact that you are carrying tension. As you tune in to what is happening in your body, you can also investigate the thoughts or emotions that are around you. Maybe those clenched fists tell you that the disagreement you had with someone is still with you. You can breathe into the tension and soften around it; and then as you let go of tension, you may find yourself also letting go of the thoughts and emotions you have unwittingly been holding onto.

Equally, if you become aware of frightening thoughts or strong emotions, you can return to your body just as it is in the here-and-now. Your body is always in the present moment, so coming back to what is happening in your body helps you to release your anxieties about the past and future.

Becoming more aware of your body also teaches you to recognize and honour your limits. As you become stressed, your body tells you that you are getting tired or that tension is building up. Mindfulness helps you to learn to listen to your body and take care of yourself before your body screams at you!

Letting Go of the Struggle

In mindfulness practice when we move up closer to what troubles us, we may begin to see that the very act of pushing our problems away leads us into constant struggle. Mindfulness suggests that we let go of the struggle and simply allow things to be as they are. There are many stresses that we cannot change, but we can let go of stressing about them. Mary's story illustrates this approach.

Mary attended mindfulness classes having developed a chronic and progressive disease. She found all of the practices really hard: she struggled with the body scan because she was in pain and restless; she struggled with the movement practice because it reminded her of all the things she could no longer do; and she struggled with the sitting practice because she just kept thinking about how awful her life had become. It was brave of her to keep coming.

Then, over halfway through the course, Mary came in looking different. She told the group with wonder that all her struggling with the practices had led to a sudden realization: she was struggling because *she was trying to live a life she no longer had.* This helped her to see how she had been adding to the stress of her illness by not accepting the changes that her illness had brought about. After that, she began to look at new ways of living her life – as it actually was now. Although there were things she was no longer able to do, she took new enjoyment in the things she *could* do, such as simply sitting quietly in her garden. In the present moment, in her garden, she felt calm and peaceful. She appreciated the plants, the sunlight and the wildlife.

Choosing Not to Believe our Thoughts

When we find ourselves in challenging or difficult situations, we can get caught up in processing events in our past and worrying about the future. We constantly run stories through our minds of all the things that might go wrong, dwelling on all possible consequences, and often imagining the worst-case scenario.

If we are late for work we might have a sequence of thoughts such as: I could have left earlier ... I should have left earlier ... I should have known that the traffic is bad on Fridays ... I'll be late for the important meeting ... My boss will be so angry! ... Perhaps I'll even lose my job ... I'd never get another job, given the current economic climate ... How will we pay the bills? I'll lose my house!

Being mindful,
we let go of struggle
and simply allow
things to be as
they are.

None of this is actually happening right now – and most of it will definitely not happen! But just thinking these thoughts, the language of these thoughts, and believing them, can create as much anxiety as if it actually *were* happening right now.

The past is over and the future has not yet happened. The present moment is often much simpler – just whatever is happening in your body, your thoughts and emotions and your world *right now*. You do not have to be imprisoned in the drama created by your thoughts – you can leave anytime you want.

Mindfulness helps us to become aware of this process in our mind and to step back to a steady place to take a wider perspective. We gradually begin to learn to recognize the "story" that we are telling ourselves and to realize that it does not necessarily tell us the truth. As we step back, or *de-centre*, we can get a clearer view of the story our thoughts are telling about ourselves and our lives. Then we can see the situation and options that are available to us.

The Power to Choose

Coming back to the present moment and being with your experience as it is, rather than as you would like it to be, may sound passive and resigned, but this is not at all the intention of mindfulness. In fact, approaching your problems with mindfulness allows you to take more skilful action when action is needed.

For example, when you are in a difficult or challenging situation, you decide, as a first step, to move out of automatic pilot and into being mode. You may choose to do this by taking a Three-Step Breathing Space (see pages 70–71). From this steadier place you can ask yourself: "What would be a wise thing to do right now?" This is the *choice-point* where you can intentionally decide between a stress reaction or a mindful stress response. You may feel sufficiently steady after doing the Three-Step Breathing Space that there is no need for further action. But if not, now would be a good time to do something that will directly address to how you are feeling.

Choosing Your Response

When you are in a stressful situation you can make choices about how to behave. It does not matter which of these options you choose – what is important is that, by choosing, you can begin to take care of yourself in such situations.

- You might choose one of the "helpful" strategies that you identified earlier, such as exercising, or talking to a friend.
- You might offer yourself kindness and reassurance in the middle of this anxiety to soothe yourself as you feel stressed.
- You might do something that gives you a sense of mastery, achievement or satisfaction, such as clearing out a drawer or answering a backlog of emails.
- You may simply choose to continue to move into your next activity mindfully, being aware of what you are doing in each moment: mindfully walking down the corridor; mindfully answering the telephone; mindfully being here.

Learning to Take Care of Yourself

Practising mindfulness can be a kindness to yourself. Becoming familiar with your habitual stress patterns, and attending to them mindfully, makes them less scary. In a way they become like old friends whom you know and understand.

Doing the practices regularly, over a period of time, can help you to be better prepared to respond when stress strikes. By becoming more aware over time you can pick up on the signals that you're stressed at an early stage, discover which responses will help you in different situations and become really intimate with helpful strategies. You can build your repertoire or toolbox of strategies through experimentation and practice. You can choose to take care of yourself.

Suzanne Kobasa, in her work on "stress hardiness", identifies the degree of control we feel we have over stress in our lives as one of the key aspects that allows us to be resilient in the face of stress. It can be really helpful to know that we have the skills and options to live wisely with whatever challenges life brings.

06

Mindfulness
in Relationships

By Eluned Gold

With mindfulness
we can choose to
focus on contact,
understanding
and love.

Connecting through Mindfulness

Relationships – whether with family, friends or the people we work with – can be among life's most consistently challenging experiences; yet the majority of us would say that they are the most important aspects of our lives.

Humans are biologically designed to form connections with their fellow beings. There are physical processes and structures within the brain and body that exist in order to develop and maintain powerful bonds with others; and not just with people we are close to – even with those we don't know. We are designed to be with other people. The following account of an incident on a train illustrates our inborn capacity to connect with others.

Christina was travelling home by train. It had been a frustrating journey. As she stepped into the carriage and took her seat, she noticed opposite her a family: a father, mother and baby girl of about 12 months old, sitting on her father's lap. As Christina sat down, the baby caught her eye and smiled at her with great openness and curiosity, as babies of that age often do. Christina smiled back as she sat down and started to look around the carriage; the baby held Christina's gaze and gave her a great big grin – she was irresistible. Christina had to grin back and as she did so she felt her body relax and open, and the tension she had been holding drained away. She recognized that in that moment she felt happy. She looked at the baby's mum and dad and they all smiled at one another. Her work done with Christina, the baby then moved her attention to somebody else in the carriage, and did the same routine with them; and that person looked at the mum and dad and also at Christina, and they all smiled. This young baby went on to work her magic until everybody in the carriage was connected. Nobody had spoken, yet all the passengers clearly experienced a sense of connection.

Attunement and Resonance

As a species we have evolved to be increasingly complex creatures, and as such we take a long time – 21 years or more – to reach maturity and independence. During these years we rely on the adults around us to protect and care for us. Our survival depends on us being able to be closely connected with our carers and fellow human beings, and on them being willing and able to stay around to care for us.

Of course our relationships amount to much more than just a survival strategy, but therein lie the *biological* roots of our capacity to connect to each other. The baby on the train demonstrated just such a capacity – by making eye contact and smiling, she invited people to notice her and to care about her. This desire for contact was reciprocated by everyone in the train carriage and triggered a desire in them for connection, so that eventually there was a connection between them as well as with the baby. One way to think about this is that the baby activated in each of the passengers their innate desire for contact. This was possible because as humans we are *biologically* designed to respond to invitations to contact and are able to signal our desire for contact to others.

We are all unique in the way that we connect with one another, and our particular style of relating to others is determined by a blend of our genetic inheritance, learned behaviours and attitudes from our parents or carers as we are growing up, and experiences that we have throughout our lives, particularly during our childhood and adolescence.

Our sense of who we are and how we relate to others develops as the people around us in our early years tune in ("attune") to us and help us to make sense of ourselves and our experiences. An important, but not necessarily frequent, experience in our lives is to feel that another person really understands what it's like to be us – this is sometimes called "resonance". Early experiences of resonance form the basis of romantic love and other relationships later in our lives.

Attunement and the corresponding experience of resonance is a two-way process. As babies we do not passively receive attunement – we actively invite it and participate in maintaining it with the adults around us, just like the baby on the train. From this early age and throughout our lives we play an active part in developing and maintaining the patterns of our own relationships.

Early relationships create a "map" for us as we grow up. Just like learning to talk (our speech and language is developed because people around us talk to us and we learn the language of our own family and culture), so we learn the way of relationships by being around our parents, carers, family and community – we see how they encourage us to relate to them and other people, and how they respond to our needs; and we quickly learn what are the spoken and unspoken "rules" in the relationships within our particular family or community.

Empathy

Empathy is the capacity to sense the inner state of another person. It is an important aspect of human relationships. Our capacity for empathy is to some extent dependent on our early experiences. However, our ability to empathize with our fellow humans is a complex process, which continues to develop throughout our lives in response to a number of varied experiences. Neuroscientists are discovering that learning mindfulness seems to increase our ability to experience and express empathy.

When we witness other people's emotions – particularly those who are close to us – we experience emotions similar to theirs. When our loved ones, partners, children, friends or colleagues describe their experiences to us, we can feel an empathic response. An example of this might be if we hear someone describe a nasty fall where they hurt themselves – we can put ourselves in their position and we momentarily feel their pain (we may even say, "Ouch"); or when someone describes their sadness at having lost a friend or relative who was dear to them, we also feel sad and perhaps even tearful. Similarly, joy, excitement and annoyance – in fact, the full range of emotions – can be infectious too.

Learning mindfulness increases our ability to experience and express empathy.

Bringing Mindfulness to Our Relationships

Much of our development as human beings is oriented toward close relationships. Given this, we may wonder why relationships can be the source of so much difficulty and disquiet.

Relationships are where our habits or patterns of thoughts, emotions and behaviours tend to show up most. As we go through life, many of these patterns remain unexamined; in other words, they are part of our set of "automatic" thoughts, feelings and behaviours. As adults we often continue to use unhelpful relationship strategies because they have become automatic and are outside of our everyday awareness.

As we discovered in Part I of this book, mindfulness is a way of bringing automatic patterns into our awareness. In theory this sounds wonderfully simple – and indeed in many ways it is – but simple is not necessarily easy (as you may already have discovered as you began to do the mindfulness practices described earlier in the book).

We may find ourselves very fixed in our automatic ways of behaving and seeing situations. In addition to this, the people around us – our partners, friends, family and work colleagues – have become used to the way that we are. They may also be very attached to us staying just the same so that we don't challenge *their* patterns of behaving and the way *they* see situations.

Any relationship is the coming together of different ways of relating and different views of the world. Sometimes we may each be waiting for the other person (or people) involved to adjust to our view of the situation. However, we don't have to wait for others to change before the pattern can be altered. There are things we can do that will affect the relationship.

Nine-Star Puzzle

Here is a pattern puzzle you can try – take a pen and try to join these nine stars using just four straight lines and without taking your pen off the paper. (For the solution, see page 184.)

How did you get on with the puzzle?

Sometimes we have to make a shift in our way of looking at things in order to see ways of connecting; we can be very attached to one viewpoint and find it difficult to view things from a different perspective. Often it is difficult to step "outside the box" and see the whole pattern.

Discovering our own Patterns

At the start of Part II, we looked at examples of the habitual relationships we may have with difficulties in our lives (see pages 74–9). Our relationships with people can show up in just the same way. Often we have developed relationship habits, which mean that we avoid being close to others; for many of us at some time in our lives, getting close may have resulted in getting hurt. If this is our experience, we are naturally cautious about becoming close again.

Do you feel that you are persistently "knocked off your feet" when something goes wrong in your relationships? When people feel insecure they will often behave in habitual but unhelpful ways to try to avoid or control the situation. The following habits are different ways in which you may avoid being close:

- Maybe you do all you can to avoid conflict, pretending there isn't a problem.
- Are you trying to fix or manage things without even telling the other person involved that there is a problem, while privately you feel upset or resentful?
- You may feel safest when you are in control, and behave aggressively around other people when you are in conflict with them. Your automatic pattern is to see relationships in terms of winners and losers, and you find it hard to be co-operative with others and to consider their point of view.

It is often very difficult for us to see our relationships clearly. We may avoid talking openly with people in our life about our relationship with them so we assume a lot without checking the reality. We may believe that others think the same way, or we may feel that we have a *right* to have our needs met by the other person in the relationship. Using mindful awareness of body sensations, emotions and thoughts, we can begin to notice our experience and see our unique patterns.

RECORDING YOUR PATTERNS OF RELATIONSHIP

Keeping a record of difficult communications over a week or two may be helpful:

- What was your first indication that this communication was feeling difficult?
- What did you notice in your body, emotions and thoughts?
- Is this a pattern you recognize?
- As you became aware things were difficult, did anything change?
- Looking back now, were there earlier indications of this difficult communication that were outside your awareness at the time?
- How long did the effects of this difficult communication stay with you?

If you keep a record you will begin to see that stressful communications can trigger off chains of thoughts and emotions. These can go on long after the event itself is over, and often fuel a sense of conflict or injustice.

By using the same skills of kindly curiosity that we have been developing in our mindfulness practice, we can learn to see the "whole pattern", viewing our own and others' role in the pattern with kindness and the courage to really look and understand. When we cultivate this *non-judging awareness* we may be already changing the patterns of our relationship – without having to do *anything*.

LEARNING TO DANCE

When we do the Aikido exercise (see page 78) in our mindfulness courses, one of the things people learn is that to "dance" you have to be in contact! That sounds obvious, but in life many of us are trying to "dance" without being really willing to get up close to the other person and to see them for who they truly are. Indeed, we are often unwilling to see *ourselves* for who *we* really are. Bringing a kindly and non-judging attitude toward ourselves and toward others, and doing our best to be willing to open up to who we and they really are, can be the first dance step.

ATTENDING TO OURSELVES FIRST

Relationships often seem to get worse when we are stressed. Attending to our own stress (see pages 98–113) may be the first step in skilful relating. Generally it is much more difficult to be effective when you are not steady and grounded yourself. For example, if someone is angry with you, it is all too easy to be reactive and to snap back or give in, rather than face the situation. It is more helpful to attend to yourself first, bringing kindly awareness to your own experience of the relationship, and to take the time to see the whole pattern, as best you can at that time. This does not mean you have to be "perfect" and need to have "conquered" all your own habits. Rather it is taking a kindly attitude toward yourself and the difficult situation you are in, and being open to whatever you may discover in this exploration and in learning to "dance".

Cultivating non-judging awareness can change the patterns of our relationships.

Getting Steady

When you notice yourself feeling fearful of approaching someone (perhaps you need to have a difficult conversation or there is a history of difficulties between you, or you just find it difficult to be close), there are some things you can do to help yourself get steady.

- Try taking a Three-Step Breathing Space (see pages 70–71) when you notice you are thinking about or planning a way to manage the person or situation.
- Spend a few moments doing a short breathing meditation (see page 57), and when you are settled, bring to mind that person and the situation. Next, "open" your awareness to include the whole picture – the pattern you are both part of. As you do this, maintain, as best you can, a kindly curiosity toward yourself, the other person and the situation.
- When you are actually face to face with someone, focus on your own experiences of body sensations – particularly the breath or feeling your feet in contact with the ground – rather than putting all your attention on the other person.

Skilful Communication

So often when we are listening to other people with the intention of being helpful, our mind is wandering somewhere else – for example, to what we have to fit into the rest of our day, what we would do in their situation, and so on. It is surprisingly difficult to just *listen*, and to be aware of the other person and what they are saying.

Mindfulness awareness helps you to stay with the situation that is occurring right here and now, which is ... *Right now I am being with this person and listening to them.*

You might like to try the Mindful Listening exercise shown opposite with a partner or friend to experience the effect of listening – and being listened to – with awareness.

Exercise: Mindful Listening

Take turns to be the one speaking and the one listening (maximum five minutes each) and have a way of timing yourselves, such as an egg-timer or stopwatch.

1 Before you start, first settle and ground yourselves with a few moments' focus on the breath.

2 When you are the listener, you simply listen, without commenting or answering or getting into a conversation. You can indicate that you are paying attention with eye contact and other non-verbal signals. Notice your own body sensations, thoughts and emotions – in particular, your own impulses to speak or your mind wandering.

3 The speaker stops when their time is up. The listener feeds back to the speaker what they have heard and understood during the mindful listening. Feedback can be about what you saw or heard.

4 Swap roles after doing a few moments' mindful breathing.

5 When you have both spoken and listened, consider:

- What was it like to be just listened to, without fear of interruption or having to justify yourself?
- For the listener, what was it like to just listen – bringing all your attention to the other person?
- During the feedback were there any surprises?
- Did your listener pick up information about you through non-verbal cues such as your body language, facial expressions or tone of voice?

When you were the listener you may have noticed thinking about what the speaker should have done or what you would have done in that situation. Listening without full attention can lead us to think we know what to do and we may start to tell the other person how to manage their problem, or even start acting to solve it. We are no longer trying to understand them; instead we have begun to act automatically as if it was us in that situation.

Whose Problem is it?

When we are faced with problems, we want to make ourselves and the other person feel better. We may react in typical ways to fix their problem and/or help them avoid the difficulty. We engage *our thinking* and in the process ignore *their feelings*. In this situation it is easy for the other person to feel judged, especially as they may already be judging themselves. By taking time to listen and by being willing to "turn toward their difficulty", we are giving the message that we have time for them and that we are willing to be with them and their difficulty, whatever it is. We are more able to be empathic. This is not the same as agreeing with them, but it demonstrates a willingness to understand the other person's point of view.

Jane left work one day feeling ashamed and anxious, having made a mistake that her boss had pointed out to her. When she arrived home in tears, her husband Peter felt moved and upset on her behalf, and immediately set about helping her find a solution to the mistake she had made. Jane was not able, at that point, to think clearly – she was still in the grip of some intense emotions.

Taking a Three-Step Breathing Space (see pages 70–71) helped them both realize what was happening. Peter was able to take a step back from wanting to fix the situation. Jane was able to ground and steady herself, while still experiencing the intensity of her emotions. They both felt connected to each other. Peter could listen as Jane described her feelings, and this was enough to help Jane realize that mistakes are inevitable, and to bring a gentle understanding to her situation.

Mindful Speaking

Skilful communication isn't just about listening and considering the other person's viewpoint. There will be times when it is important for us to express our own opinions, needs and wants. This can be particularly difficult if we are in disagreement with someone or we want to tell them about their upsetting or unhelpful behaviour. Here are some suggestions to help with mindful speaking:

- Give yourself time to consider what you want to say, taking time out so that you can *respond* to the situation rather than *reacting*.
- Speak about your own experience of the situation rather than what the other person has done.
- Focus on your own experiences of body sensations throughout the conversation.
- Using the following "formula" can help you avoid getting into accusations and recriminations: "When you do A, I feel B, and I would like you to do C instead."

Are You Who I Think You Are?

When we first meet someone, we are often very quick to judge and form a first impression. We very rarely revise this first impression, especially if it seems generally correct.

Our minds tend to look for patterns, so when we meet someone we are inclined to fit them into a model that already exists in our mind. For example, someone may remind us of a person from our past – perhaps a parent or school teacher. If this previous relationship has been negative or stressful, we are more likely to remember it. We do this even with people we've known for a long time.

When the relationship becomes difficult, we are even more inclined to fall back on negative assumptions and preconceived ideas about the person. This can lead us to consider the person to be unsatisfactory. Once this has happened we often find ourselves wishing the person would be different. Mindfulness helps us remember we can *choose* where to focus our attention. We can focus on what we find unsatisfactory in the other person *or* we can focus on contact, understanding and love. We strengthen what we focus on.

When our minds are not cluttered with old habits and assumptions about ourselves and the people we are with, we are able to be fully open to the relationship with the person we have right now in this present moment, with all its rich mixture of ease and difficulty. Mindful awareness helps us see ourselves and others clearly, rather than through a series of "filters" or fogs.

07

Mindfulness
with Children

By Eluned Gold

Teaching our children
to manage difficulties
with gentleness
is a loving gift we
can offer them.

Getting Started

This chapter is called "Mindfulness *with* Children", and not "Mindfulness *for* Children", because the best way to introduce mindfulness to children is to be mindful *with* them. We know that children learn best from the adults who care for them, and that they take in far more from watching and copying than they do from simply being told what to do.

Children are naturally mindful and are often spontaneously in touch with a non-judging sense of wonder, curiosity and joy toward the world. As we know, mindfulness is learned through the experience of it rather than being told about it. So, if you are developing your own mindfulness practice and bringing mindfulness into your everyday interactions with your children, they are likely to be picking up mindful attitudes. Of course, we can extend this by teaching children some specific ways in which to be mindful and by inviting them to join us in our mindfulness practices and activities.

Research tells us that the very structure of our brain develops in response to our experiences, and this development is very rapid in early childhood and adolescence so the experiences we are exposed to then help literally to shape the brain. It is important to have a sense of perspective about this. Naturally, we want to protect our children, and to see them develop as kind, independent and compassionate individuals. However, we also know that life brings us hardship and even harm from time to time, and teaching our children to manage difficulties with gentleness is a loving gift we can offer them.

They will best learn this from the attitudes and actions of the adults around them. When we are mindfully aware ourselves, then we are more able to "tune in to" or "attune" to our children in a way that will help them make sense of their internal experiences, their relationship with others and the world in general. "Attunement" from parents or caregivers can influence brain development.

Never Too Early

So, when and how can we introduce mindfulness to our children? In some ways it's never too early – there are mindfulness programmes to help parents prepare for birth, and once your baby has arrived the opportunities for practising mindfulness are plentiful – for example, through mindful baby bathing, or mindful walking when you have a crying baby late at night.

As babies grow into children, it is not always straightforward to decide whether they are developmentally ready to learn some of these practices. It is important to be guided by the child and your own intuitions when assessing their readiness. It is also important to recognize if we are being motivated by our own goal – for example, we may be feeling helpless in the face of their distress. In these situations it is really important to be guided by what is helpful for the child.

One way of explaining the concept of mindfulness to children is with a "snow globe". An agitated mind, when we can't think clearly, is like a shaken-up snow globe when we can't see the figures inside. If we wait calmly, focusing on our breath for a few breaths, the "snow" settles and we can see clearly. The "snow" hasn't gone away but it has settled enough for us to see what we are dealing with.

A Few Tips

Keep practices short and age-appropriate and above all bring trust and patience to the process – there is no need to rush! A rule of thumb is one minute of practice for each year of age. This is not a goal – simply a general guideline. Your 15-year-old might do best with a five-minute practice, rather than a 15-minute one. The best way to introduce mindfulness practice to children is through play. Playing is a child's natural route to openness and curiosity – exactly the qualities encouraged in mindfulness. Some useful pointers: never insist that a child meditates; keep practices short; start gradually and be patient; encourage curiosity and openness by being curious and open yourself; *make it FUN and be creative.*

Tuning in

"Tuning in" can be a good way to help your child understand that the skill of mindful awareness is to be able to focus on a chosen object or field of attention, stay with it and notice when the mind has wandered; then to gently return your attention to the chosen focus.

It is about simply noticing what is here, without trying to change anything.

Tuning in to the Breath

This is perhaps one of the most versatile of the mindfulness practices for children. Susan Kaiser Greenland in her book *The Mindful Child* describes how she has children in nursery lie down with a soft toy on their tummy, and encourages them to focus on the breath, watching the toy gently move up and down as if they were rocking it to sleep.

In any of the breathing practices, with younger children you can point out that they are choosing where to place their attention, and that focusing on the breath may change how they are breathing – often slowing and steadying the breath. This might result in them feeling calmer and more relaxed. With older children and teens it is generally more helpful to let them try this and discover the changes for themselves, encouraging them to reflect on their experience.

For some children (and adults) the breath might not be a comfortable focus – for example, a child with asthma or other breathing difficulties; or a child who has experienced panic attacks. It is important not to force them to keep the attention on the breath if it is not comfortable; finding a place in the body where they can hold their attention comfortably (maybe the soles of the feet or in the hands) may take some experimentation. Often, people who have been given an alternative to the breath to start with find they can gradually bring their attention back to the breath if they choose to.

Exercise: Tuning in to the Breath

A good way of introducing your child to their breath is to use a windmill. Children learn that they can control the breath – blowing soft and hard. They can notice that they are still breathing, even when they are not aware of it. They can choose to pay attention to the breath or not – it is always there! This idea also works for blowing bubbles or even a dandelion so long as your child is old enough to have the breath control. Older children may choose to notice the sensations of the breath in other parts of the body, as in the adult practices (see page 57).

Placing the hands on the belly is another way of helping children tune in to their breath as they watch their hands rise and fall.

Counting breaths is another great way to bring awareness to the breath, as well as to the present moment. Counting occupies the mind, which makes it easier to focus.

1 Choose a number that is more than easily manageable for your child (for example, 3, 5 or 8).

2 With hands on the belly, your child counts on each out-breath up to the agreed number, focusing the mind on the breath and the belly. Alternatively, you can count for them.

3 Once the desired number is reached, simply start again.

4 Once your child is used to this, they can begin to recognize when the mind has wandered; therefore, a development of this practice is to return to 1 each time the they notice the mind has wandered.

This practice, done for a short time, can be fun and is often wonderfully calming whenever your child is feeling upset or unsettled. Breathing with your child can also be helpful.

Tuning in to the Body

Children are naturally curious. You can invite exploration by simply asking them to place a hand on their own knee or elbow and feel the workings of the joint as it moves around. It is then a short step to ask them to contemplate what the joint feels like from the inside, without placing a hand there. As your child becomes used to placing attention in different parts of the body and noticing sensations, whether the sensations arise from external sources like touch or temperature, or internal sources like tingling or throbbing, you are gradually introducing them to the Body Scan. Using a torch beam you can illustrate the idea of narrow- and wide-beam focus. Narrow-beam might be a toe; wide-beam, the whole leg or even the whole body.

You can also bring your child's attention to their body in movement through activities such as mindful walking, running, dancing and football.

The Body Scan

A fun way to introduce the Body Scan to children is for them to lie on a large sheet of paper while you draw slowly around their body, bringing their attention to each part of the body as your pen moves past it. You can invite your child to tell you what sensations they are noticing: an itchy foot, a warm leg, a tickly knee, and so on. If this becomes a favourite practice, you might begin to have your child reflect on their experiences in silence. Your child may insist that they draw around you. This is an excellent way to model the kind of experiences and sensations that they might be noticing. If the exercise results in giggling and squirming, enjoy having fun and very gently return your child's attention to the purpose of the practice, which is to pay attention to their body in a deliberate way, in a wide or narrow focus – just like the torch beam.

This can be a useful practice when your child needs to relax. For example, a brief guided Body Scan (see page 177) when they are in bed and preparing for sleep can be a wonderful way to help them settle after the busy-ness of the day.

Tuning in to the Senses

Children can be encouraged to pay attention to their senses simply as part of everyday life, by taking a moment to look at colours, smell food and listen to the birds. Children will also enjoy the Eating Mindfully exercise (see pages 49–50). All these are ways to use awareness to enrich their world.

Exercise: The Fruit Game

Here is a game that most children like, which uses all the senses except seeing. We are so used to experiencing our world visually that using our other senses can heighten our awareness. This can be done with a small group of three or more children. You will need one lemon per child (it can also be done with potatoes, oranges, and so on).

1 Ask all players to close their eyes, or tie a scarf around their eyes as a blindfold.

2 The children take one lemon each, and carefully examine it, feeling its size, shape and texture, smelling it and even tasting it. (You might want to guide this, giving instructions every so often to keep everyone focused.) This can last two to four minutes, depending on the age of the children.

3 Collect all of the lemons and place them back in the bowl, but all jumbled up.

4 Now, invite each child to identify his or her particular lemon. (Most of us believe that we'll never be able to do this. But, in fact, through using our senses, we have become very familiar with our own special lemon, and often we find we are easily able to identify our own one.

Tuning in to Thoughts and Emotions

Tuning in to awareness of our thoughts and emotions can be quite a difficult concept, even for adults. Once we have learned how to notice them, we can clearly understand the power that our thoughts and emotions have over our lives. Of course we should also let children know that not all thinking is bad – working things out, imagination and day-dreaming are all important aspects of our being who we are. Thinking is only troublesome when it leads us into feeling bad or when we drift away at times when we should be paying attention. These are the times that learning to "tune in" can really help us – one boy who was learning mindfulness at school said it helped him because he heard what the teacher said and didn't have to keep asking to hear it again.

Thoughts are like monkeys leaping about in trees – they don't stay in one place and they tell us stories, which aren't always true. Sometimes, when all the "thought-monkeys" link up, they can lead us far away from our true experience.

Emotions can often be noticed as body sensations, which children can be helped to tune in to, name and welcome – even unpleasant or very intense ones. When things are intense or we feel "wobbly", we can choose to tune in to sensations in the body, or we can tune in to the breath to settle and calm ourselves.

Seeing emotions described in this way and located in the body can help children manage their feelings. When children can give experiences a name – like "sadness", "anger" or "happiness" – it helps them understand that these things are part of our everyday experience of life to be acknowledged. Tuning in to emotions in this way can be a good starting point for choosing how to deal with things.

Exploring all experience with kindness helps us to understand our own habitual thoughts, feelings and actions. Kindness can help us to spot these habits in a gentle and accepting way, without wanting things to be different or racing for a solution. Children can be helped to tune in to kindness, by asking them to recall what they felt like when someone was kind to them, or when they were kind to someone else. Tuning in to kindness is a way to move toward wise action, finding gentle ways to be kind to ourselves, other people and the planet.

Helping with Difficulty

Children experience difficulties in their lives, just as adults do. Often they do not have the resources and experience to deal with difficulty, and need the help of the adults around them. Equally, they may not have built up strong habits of shutting out and moving away from difficulty, which as adults we often do. Using the skills of "tuning in" that we've been exploring earlier in this chapter, we can teach children more skilful ways to deal with inevitable difficulties in their lives.

Your own attitude of patience, acceptance and kindness will do much to encourage similar attitudes in your child. It is important to recognize that children often show their distress through their behaviour. So if your child is so-called "behaving badly", exploring sensations, emotions and thoughts, and tuning in to kindness, can often give them a way to express and understand things they may have been struggling with.

One way to do this is to create an Awareness Chart (see opposite) on a sheet of unlined paper. Draw four boxes, and label them Body Sensations, Emotions, Thoughts and Kindness (see opposite). By writing down or drawing your child's experiences in the relevant box you can see that all of these elements interact – they can't really be separated, although it can be helpful, when we are "tuning in" to them, to look at them in turn, as it helps us to really get to know and be friends with all aspects of our experience. This chart can be used in different ways with children of different ages. Younger children might enjoy making and decorating their own chart, which they can return to again and again. Prepared dots or stickers with familiar body sensations, feelings and thoughts written on them may be helpful. You can include some blanks for unique experiences. Older children can create their own charts whenever they want to explore an experience.

Johann, his mum and his little brother Peter had recently moved to a new town, after his mum and dad's separation. Johann was having trouble making friends in his new school. The situation was getting worse and worse, and Johann was becoming withdrawn and not wanting to go to school. Choosing her moment carefully, Johann's mum asked Johann if he wanted to talk. She listened carefully, helping Johann to calm himself using hands-on belly breath awareness, and together they made some space to explore Johann's experience in school that day.

Powerful Difficulties

Sometimes children experience difficulties and situations that feel particularly serious. Difficulties can seem so big and dark that it feels as though there is no way out. At these times it can be very frightening to turn toward difficulty.

Awareness Chart

BODY SENSATIONS
• Tears
• Heart beating
• Butterflies in tummy

THOUGHTS
• I'll never have any friends
• I'll never be any good
• Nobody likes me
• I can't be happy

Tuning in

EMOTIONS
• Confusion
• Fear • Anger
• Sadness

KINDNESS
• The world
• Self
• Others

Exercise: Understanding a Dark Spot

The following activity can be a helpful way for children to come to understand that a problem is not all dark but has different aspects and qualities.

1 Take a sheet or two of kitchen paper and make a dark spot in the centre of it by applying five or six different coloured felt pens on top of one another, leaving the tips on the paper until the colour soaks in.

2 Gently drip some water onto the dark spot – *this is like applying a clear view of mindfulness to our dark spot.*

3 Quite soon you will see that the colours separate out. It's the same when you pay mindful attention to your difficulties – you start to see them for what they are and, in this clear-sightedness, the difficulty seems more manageable.

4 The colours in the dark spot will continue to separate out until it's no longer a dark spot but a whole range of different colours.

This is when attuned listening from the adults around children is necessary. Children will feel most supported by the people who love and know them best, and your role is important. However, there may be times when it's important to seek professional help as well – perhaps from a doctor, psychologist or therapist.

When we have powerful difficulties, it can feel like a dark spot that is so big there appears to be little room in our lives for anything else. Tuning in mindfully, particularly to our bodies, can help us step outside of the dark spot and see it for what it is. Often the Three-Step Breathing Space (see pages 70–71) can help us take this step. We can find a steady place to see things clearly and from here see that other things in our life that are fine, but have been hidden because all we have

been seeing is the dark spot. This won't make the dark spot go away, but will nevertheless give us a chance to see that it's not the only thing in our lives – thereby changing our relationship to it. We may also notice that it's not all dark, but is made up of many different aspects and qualities.

Sonia was 12 years old and was very close to her grandfather. When he died after a short illness, Sonia found it extremely difficult to come to terms with the loss.

At first she kept very busy, but later found herself often feeling quarrelsome. After some time, Sonia's dad asked her if she would like to learn about mindfulness. He taught her how to "tune in" to her breath, body, emotions and kindness. This helped her to understand and manage her emotions a little better. When Sonia's dad encouraged her to draw her own "dark spot", Sonia was able to see that she had been living in the dark spot. Even when she was being busy, all she could see was the loss of her grandfather. Using mindfulness to help her to step outside the "dark spot", she could notice that there were other things in her life.

Using the Understanding a Dark Spot exercise (opposite), Sonia could recognize the different aspects of her grief: sadness, fear, anger, keeping busy (to keep feelings at bay) and hopelessness. All these were part of her grief experience. So, although the mindful awareness hadn't made the grief disappear, seeing it for what it was – and realizing that she was not alone with it – helped Sonia develop a different way of being with her grief, rather than being stuck inside it.

Learning from Our Children

Children have not built up the entrenched habits of thoughts, emotions and behaviours that we adults have. Adults can learn a lot from children's courage and willingness to explore their experiences with great enthusiasm and openness. Children are spontaneously generous, kind and a lot of fun. By introducing them to mindfulness, and teaching them how to tune in to their own experience, we can help them continue to bring these wonderful qualities into their lives.

08

Mindfulness
for Carers

By Vanessa Hope

Bringing mindfulness to moments during our day can give us small oases of steadiness and perhaps even peace, allowing us the opportunity to let go of the cares that do not easily let go of us.

How Mindfulness Can Help

We looked earlier in this book at how levels of stress have increased in the 21st century. The same can be said about the number of people now needing care. With a growing elderly population, there are many carers working in residential services; but there are many more who are full-time carers looking after members of their own family at home. The people being cared for – husbands, wives, parents and children – may have had a life-changing accident, they may have a progressive illness or they may be reaching the end of their life. Carers live with an incredible amount of stress, and it is only fairly recently that this has begun to be recognized.

While each carer is an individual, carers share certain similar difficulties. There are many *physical* demands of care work such as feeding, dressing, changing, moving and lifting someone who may be unable to do these things for themselves, managing the necessary equipment needed for medical or care needs, and coping with reduced or interrupted sleep.

There are also significant *emotional* demands. For example, roles may have changed significantly within the family as you juggle various demands on your time. The person you care for may now be very different from the person you knew before. It may also be stressful and frustrating communicating with someone who perhaps has limited ability to understand and respond, or who may not even recognize you. You may well have to manage your own frustration and anger, perhaps even aggression, as well as that of the person you care for. You may be constantly tired and worried, and as a result become irritable and resentful. In this very challenging role it is easy to feel that you are not caring well enough and therefore feel guilty.

If you are a full-time carer these difficulties may be magnified. Being a carer can feel relentless. You must be available 24 hours a day. You need to be constantly vigilant. In many cases there is no foreseeable end to the need for care, and the situation could deteriorate. This leads to uncertainty about the future and often to financial difficulties. There can be a constant struggle to communicate with social services, consultants and hospitals. You can feel isolated and alone.

It is very understandable that carers can become burnt out or depressed. This is why it is important to find effective ways to live well with these challenges and to care for yourself in the midst of so many demands. Given that mindfulness training is intended to help people turn toward difficulties in their lives and begin to find ways to live alongside these difficulties, it is not surprising that mindfulness seems to have much to offer to both those who work as carers and to those who care for family at home.

Living in the Moment

As a carer, perhaps more than many people, you may really understand the importance of being in the present moment, simply doing what has to be done moment by moment. However, you maybe usually do this in the service of others. It can be really difficult to manage to find time for yourself. Mindfulness training can help you to focus on this moment as a way to nurture yourself.

In the Eating Mindfully exercise (see pages 49–50), you were encouraged to experiment with eating a piece of fruit slowly and with great attention. People often find that paying close attention like this can transform an otherwise mundane activity into a space to nourish themselves, not just with food, but with time and care. How often, during our busy lives, do we move out of our constant doing and allow ourselves simply to be? But bringing mindfulness to moments during our day can give us small oases of steadiness and perhaps even peace, allowing us the opportunity to let go of the cares that do not easily let go of us.

Cherish the Moment – Cherish Yourself

You might like to try some of the following suggestions:

- Simply feel the sensations of sitting down, coming to rest, with your feet on the floor and your body supported by the chair.
- Feel the flow of your movement from one place to another in the house as you go about your caring tasks.
- Take time to mindfully enjoy a cup of tea or coffee or a refreshing cold drink.
- Choose something tasty to eat.
- Spend just five minutes sitting in the garden feeling the air on your skin and listening to the birds.

Another possibility is to do a routine activity mindfully, allowing yourself to:

- Really experience all the sensations of having a shower or bath.
- See, and perhaps actually appreciate, the colours of the bubbles or the sparkle of newly-washed dishes as you wash up.
- Feel the sunshine on your skin as you hang out the washing or mow the grass.

As best you can, keep it simple. If you regularly bring mindful awareness to ordinary activities like those in the box, above, for short periods of time, they become part of your routine. In this way throughout your day you can begin to weave some much-needed nourishment into your life.

Living in the moment can have other far-reaching results. By the very nature of their problem, carers often find that they are constantly caught up in thoughts about the past or the future. You may look back, often with great sadness, on how life used to be when your loved one was well. You may also, naturally, worry about what the future will bring. And even your thoughts about this moment may be judgmental and critical about your ability to cope with the situation or about your caring skills.

Mindfulness practice, however, helps us to anchor ourselves in the present moment and to give our full attention to what is actually here. As we learn to pause and see our experience more clearly, we can begin to see how our thoughts and feelings and the way we act may add to this already difficult life we're living.

In this way we become more able to accept our experience as it is and to find steadiness by letting go of the struggle of wanting things to be different. This in no way implies resignation or giving in. Seeing our situation clearly is just the first step that enables us to make wise choices about how to act and respond.

Showing Kindness Toward Ourselves

Maybe you can begin to see how mindfulness practice is a way of being gentle and kind toward yourself. As we cherish ourselves in moments of our day and allow ourselves to be as we are – no matter what thoughts or emotions pass through – we are befriending ourselves rather than criticizing or judging ourselves.

Knowing your Limits

As we practise mindfulness, we begin to see the reality of our lives – not how we would like it to be or how it should be, but how it actually is. We also begin to understand ourselves better and to recognize when we come up against our limits. This is especially obvious in the mindful movement practices. As we hold our arms up above our heads, for example, we become aware of their weight, of tingling in our fingers and sometimes the desire to bring our arms down.

We tend to have one of two reactions to this desire. One is to immediately pull out of the stretch; the other is to grit our teeth and hold it. These are normal human reactions. In our lives we constantly choose between pulling back from these challenges and pushing ourselves on. It is sometimes only when we have gone too far and exhausted ourselves that we realize that we have gone beyond our limits, and maybe have done so for a very long time.

Mindfulness teaches us to respond to the experience of being at our limits with gentleness and compassion

The practice of bringing mindful awareness to our lives begins to develop our sensitivity to this "edge". We begin to identify the subtle (and not so subtle!) signs that allow us to challenge ourselves appropriately without pushing ourselves too far. As we practise mindfulness, we begin to see the reality of our situation – not how we would like it to be or how it should be, but how it actually is.

Jim's wife had had a stroke, which left her very unsteady on her feet. She only went out shopping if Jim was there to support her, because she felt embarrassed using a stick. Sometimes, after these outings, Jim would suffer from backache, but he never knew when or how bad it would be. During the mindful movement practice on his mindfulness course, Jim became aware of his back starting to twinge in certain positions. He began to understand which movements his back didn't like and how to move in a way that didn't create a twinge. He saw how he was holding himself to ward off the twinge, and found that this tightening added to his pain.

The next time he was out walking with his wife, Jim noticed similar sensations in his back and, instead of carrying on, he told her that he was in discomfort and asked her if she would mind using her stick for a while. She was happy to help, and this prevented his backache becoming worse. His ability to notice the signals from his body started to filter into the rest of Jim's life – like honouring how tired he was in the evenings and allowing himself to leave tasks that were not pressing until morning.

Mindfulness in Communication

Jim's example leads us to another aspect of mindfulness training that carers find supportive. Carers spend much of their time being involved in difficult communications with other people: the person they care for, doctors, consultants, social workers and those who deal with finances through government benefits or insurance. This can add huge amounts of stress to an already stressful life. For more on communication please see the Relationships chapter.

Exercise: Kindly Awareness Meditation

This short meditation practice is a way you can be friendly to yourself.

1 Find a quiet place where you can sit comfortably with your back straight and your feet firmly on the ground. Sense the support of this posture and of the floor and the chair.

2 Hold yourself and your experience of sitting here with kindness and gentleness (maybe a sense of being your own good friend).

3 Begin by bringing your attention to any sense of ease that you find ... noticing any *pleasant* sensations in your body: the touch of air, warmth, coolness ... holding these sensations in awareness, resting here.

4 Notice the places where there are no particular sensations, places which feel *neutral* ... just allowing your experience to be as it is.

5 Now escort your attention to any areas of the body where there is *discomfort or intensity* – maybe aching or tension or numbness, acknowledging that these sensations are there ... and noticing your reactions to them (perhaps a bracing or pushing away) ... cradling these reactions with kindly awareness too.

6 Now as you sit and hold all of these sensations (pleasant, neutral, difficult) in friendly awareness ... notice how they may come and go or change ... and how your thoughts and emotions also come and go and change along with them ... be aware of maybe wanting the pleasurable sensations to stay and the discomfort to go, and that you are possibly simply ignoring the neutral places. Without trying to change anything just be with yourself as you are and surround yourself and your experience with kindly awareness.

7 Return your attention to sitting here on the chair, your feet firm against the ground ... sitting with a firm and solid base, just as you are in this moment. And now take this friendliness toward yourself into the next moments of your day.

One of the weekly home practices on the mindfulness course asks the group to look at the difficult communications that they find in their lives. We don't do this with a view to problem-solving each item but rather in order to begin to see the *patterns of reaction* that can influence how we communicate with, and interact with, other people in our lives. Communication is a two-way process, which unfolds in ways that are dependent on what each participant does.

Seeing Your Patterns of Reaction

Why not try this questionnaire for yourself? Think of a few occasions recently when it has been stressful communicating with someone. Ask yourself these questions:

- What emotions were present for you?
- What thoughts, images and memories were there for you as this happened?
- What was happening in your body?
- What were your reactions and behaviours toward the other person … and toward yourself?
- What do you notice as you explore these memories now?
- What patterns do you notice? Are you someone who explodes? Or do you find it hard to state your point of view? Perhaps you tend to avoid talking about problems. Do you sometimes react in one way and sometimes in another? And does this maybe depend on the situation itself or the person you are interacting with?

As you look at your reactions in these difficult situations, maybe one of the following two stories from carers who have come to mindfulness courses rings true for you? Both demonstrate how mindfulness can help us to get in touch with our feelings and also perhaps soften toward the people with whom we are communicating when they are perhaps presenting challenging behaviour. But mindfulness can also help us to stand our ground when we need to.

Tracey had become the full-time carer for her mother, who was recovering from a stroke that had left her partially paralyzed. Helping her mother to dress and feed herself was not easy but they managed pretty well together.

However, following a second stroke her mother was unable to do anything for herself and Tracey had to arrange for a team of carers to come into the house and help her. Her mother's bedroom became filled with technology, including a special bed and a hoist to lift her in and out of it. The care team were well-meaning but they were overstretched with a lot of other people to look after. This meant that Tracey never knew when they would arrive, and they were often in a rush to get on to the next client.

The schedule had been arranged so that Tracey could continue to go to her art class – the one time during the week when she could get out and do something to nourish herself. However, the care team often arrived too late for her to go. Tracey became increasingly upset and angry about this state of affairs, but she felt that her morning away from care duties was not important enough to make a big fuss about it.

Eventually, however, she decided that because of the way she was feeling she had to say something. She found herself getting agitated and rehearsing over and over again what she should say and how to say it. She felt herself shaking and noticed how shallow her breathing was.

Then she remembered the Mountain Meditation (see page 176), which she had learned on her mindfulness course and which had taught her how to notice the qualities of a mountain in herself. She felt her feet firm against the floor, rooted in the earth, sensing herself as tall, strong and standing her ground.

Tracey began to really sense her frustration and to fully acknowledge how much she needed this precious time to herself. From this steadier place, she told the care team that she could see how busy they were but that the art class was a really important lifeline for her. They were taken aback by the intensity of her feelings but nevertheless were sympathetic and agreed that they would try to time their arrival so that she could get to her class.

Laura cares for her 20-year-old son Dan, who had a motorcycle accident two years ago. He is now in a wheelchair, and injury to his brain means that this previously easy-going young man is now prone to dramatic mood swings, made worse by the fact that he does not always understand what is being said. Sometimes communicating with him in a way that means he can understand and help with the simplest tasks seems impossible. Laura can feel at her wits' end.

One day, Laura had to get Dan in from the garden early to go for a hospital appointment. He often got angry at having to stop what he was doing and did not understand why the appointment was important. As she steeled herself for an argument, Laura paused and took a breathing space. She came in touch with how she was bracing herself for a battle. As she stayed with this tightness, she became aware of a heavy feeling around her heart and found that underneath her frustration was immense sadness for herself and for the strongly individual little boy her son had once been. She felt the tightness dissolve and she gently put her arm around him, saying: "Time to go in now, Dan, and get ready for your hospital appointment." To her surprise, he hugged her back. Laura then realized how often just expecting confrontation made the situation worse. She also realized that it was the first time for a while that she had simply given her son a hug, and how good that simple, wordless communication felt.

Asking for Support

It can be incredibly difficult to admit we need support. We may feel this is an admission of failure, and also worry that getting help will reduce our ability to control our situation. It can be very hard having carers working – and sometimes even staying – in our home, and not knowing who will arrive … or when. Normal life and privacy are compromised and the helpers may be people whom we do not find particularly sympathetic or even nice to have around.

It can be very easy to let go of the activities and connections in our lives that really support us, as we focus on caring for someone else. During the

mindfulness course, we are encouraged to bring our awareness to what nurtures us and what drains us, and to look at ways of putting more nourishing, connecting and inspiring activities into our lives. (See Hot Air Balloon exercise, page 173).

One important discovery that we can make is that others may be really important in helping us to take care of ourselves. As we saw from Tracey's story (see page 155), mindfulness helps us to find a steady place from which to express our needs and ask for this support.

This illustrates the importance of turning toward our difficulties (one of the key skills learned in mindfulness). It is only when we are able to turn toward our difficulties and acknowledge how things are for us that we can make wise choices. This was what helped Tracey to express her own needs when talking to the care team, and also helped Laura to soften toward her son and make a gesture

Professional
support

Leisure and nourishment
Community, friends and family

A sense of meaning in life experiences,
supported by mindful awareness

We need layers of support, like a pyramid. It is the bottom layer that gives us the foundation on which to build the rest.

of love, rather than allowing her habitual reaction of frustration and irritation to take over. If we do not admit to painful feelings such as sadness and anger we can risk letting these fester or cut us off from the affection and the help that we need.

Humour and Laughter

Many people who come to a mindfulness group say that it has been important to meet people like themselves, who share similar experiences and problems. This is especially true for groups that have as much in common as carers do. It is wonderful to find that others get frustrated and lose their tempers and then blame themselves just as we do. And who else can understand the complexities of a cocktail of medications or being dependent on strangers, other than someone who does it too? The sharing on a mindfulness course often leads to support, but it can also lead to laughter as carers begin to hold their common day-to-day problems more lightly, as part of being human.

Laughter can be healing in itself, but it is also a mark of something more important. When we are able to laugh at ourselves and at our problems, we are inevitably stepping back and taking a wider perspective on them. The humour that so often arises on the mindfulness courses has its roots not only in shared life experience but also in the actual practices that the group is engaged in. These help us to see our minds at work, often leading to wry humour at how we can get caught up in the same story time and again. This ability to laugh gently with, rather than at, ourselves allows us to stop taking ourselves and our problems so personally and seriously. Our problems are seen as part of the ebb and flow of our lives and not as something that defines us – and this can be very healing.

As we practise mindfulness we realize that, just like other human beings, we are doing our best in often very difficult circumstances. We begin to understand that we are not alone in our struggles (however isolated we may feel at times). And, as our confidence in the support of the practices grows, we can begin to trust that we can bring more kindness and wisdom into our lives.

09.

Mindfulness
and Illness

By Sarah Silverton

Mindfulness can allow us to see things more clearly and respond skilfully and wisely when we are ill.

How We Experience Illness

Over the course of a year, most of us will catch the odd cough or cold. We may find ourselves laid low for a day or two, but the virus passes and we soon forget about it. If we are lucky enough to be generally healthy, we probably feel reasonably well most of the time. However, it is surprising how even a minor illness can have quite an effect on our lives. You might imagine that the impact an illness has on us would directly relate to its seriousness, but actually the factors that come into play are quite complex. How we think and feel, and what we do about being ill, can make a great difference to the experience.

As well as the physical effects of illness, there are also thoughts and feelings about being ill. We may feel anger, resentment, frustration or fear. We are likely to be anxious, and even depressed, guilty or ashamed. Our minds and our bodies are so interconnected that one directly affects the other. So we feel ill, and the mind starts analyzing the situation, perhaps replaying the past, creating stories about what might happen *if...*, as well as organizing and planning for the future.

It may be helpful to think of illness as being like an arrow that hits us and hurts us. The symptoms really exist, and we may or may not be able to influence their impact with treatment or surgery. We may experience discomfort or pain and tiredness or fatigue, and this may be short-lived or of a long duration. We may know that we will recover in time, or we may be unsure of how things will be for us in the future. How we react to this situation will determine whether there is a second arrow. This new arrow represents our thoughts about the condition and our emotional and physical reactions: the meaning of the illness for us. This second arrow can be equally – if not more – painful for us.

We have already explored elsewhere in the book how, as human beings, we react to situations that we find unpleasant and to things that we want to be different. We are designed to pull away from that which causes us pain and to try to get rid of threatening situations. So, while this reaction is to be expected for all of us as human beings and is intended to help us cope with difficulty, through awareness we see how our reaction may actually be making things worse.

Feeling rage and resentment about our situation may well add to the tightness in our body, thereby fuelling our pain or fatigue. If we feel very tired or we are in pain, we are much more likely to have gloomy or worrying thoughts. We may expend vast amounts of energy fighting against the reality of our experience (through denial or repeated efforts to fix).

How Mindfulness Can Help

Mindfulness can help us discover how best to take care of ourselves, given life is difficult just now. It allows us to see things more clearly and to find ways to respond skilfully and wisely to the difficult situation that we find ourselves in when we are ill, whatever our illness.

On the face of it, it seems unlikely that mindfulness could provide protection against illnesses such as the common cold. However, research by Richard Davidson (see page 22) has found that people who practise mindfulness regularly may indeed have improved immunity to viruses. So it seems that mindfulness may be able to make a difference to the first arrow as well as to the second one.

It can sometimes be hard to separate the first and second arrows in our experience amid the turmoil of sensations, thoughts and feelings. Which are the aspects of our situation that we are able to influence and which are those that we can't? Mindfulness practice can help us to see things as clearly as is possible at these times.

Mindfulness can help us discover how best to take care of ourselves, given this is how things are now.

Danielle was 28 and travelled to work each day on the train. She had an 18-month-old daughter, Zoë, who attended a nursery and seemed to pick up every bug going. "I've never had so many colds in my life," Danielle told her mother. "It seems to take me longer and longer to get over them. I just feel exhausted and worn out – and I'm really worried about the effect on Zoë."

For Danielle, it was clear that the colds themselves were not the only problem. True, she had some nasty physical symptoms. It may well have been appropriate for her to take some cold remedies to help ease her symptoms and support her immunity. (This would have been responding to the first arrow; see page 162.) But Danielle also found that she was worrying a lot: "What if I keep getting ill? What if I'm so ill that I can't go to work and I lose my job? What if I am so ill that I can't look after Zoë anymore? I've got all these colds because Zoë is at nursery when she should be home with me ... It's all my fault."

Danielle realized that one of the reasons why she felt so exhausted was that she worried about things. Currently she was anxious about her health and the consequences of her health problems, especially when she lay in bed at night. This made it much harder for her to get the sleep she knew she needed – and she worried about that too. Having started with a common cold – nasty as it was while it lasted – Danielle was now adding to her cold symptoms all sorts of really unpleasant thoughts and feelings, which directly affected her sleep. (This was the second arrow; see page 162.)

Danielle discovered that she could come back to noticing her breath over and over throughout the day. She noticed that she was worrying less, she was not letting her thoughts run so far, and was also sleeping better. By choosing to do two simple exercises, Pausing in our Lives (see page 166) and Body Breathing (see page 168), Danielle began to learn to step out of habitual patterns of thinking and to stand in a steadier place, where she was more aware and present in her life. The colds were no longer such a problem because she was able to deal with the physical symptoms and she was letting go of the extra arrow of worrying, seeing everything as a catastrophe, and judging herself.

Exercise: Pausing in our Lives

It helps to keep the following exercise very simple and brief. You are not doing anything other than stopping and noticing what is going on with friendly interest – just for a few moments – and then you can carry on with whatever you were doing. Practising this exercise regularly a few times every day can help you develop the habit of stepping back and moving out of autopilot to be with yourself right here.

You might choose to practise pausing in your life every time you engage in a certain routine activity, such as: boiling the kettle, washing your hands, eating a meal, waiting for the computer to boot up, doing the dishes, leaving the house or getting into the car.

You might also choose to practise pausing whenever you notice you are "off balance" and feeling speedy, anxious, stressed, irritable or upset.

- Begin by *stopping* what you are doing (shifting mental gears from doing to being) and then ask yourself one of the following questions:

- What is going on for me at the moment?
- What am I noticing right now?

Remember that this pause is about noticing – it's not about analyzing or getting rid of any experiences you notice, that you don't like or want.

Exercise: Body Breathing

This practice can be done anywhere, but works particularly well when we're in bed – for example, when we're awake at night and with a mind racing with thoughts, or when we are ill and needing to stay in bed.

1 Feel the sensations of the contact of your body with the bed and experience the feel of the bedding over you and the pillow under your head.

2 Become aware of the fact that you are breathing, letting the breath breathe itself, without needing to change it. Simply feel the breath coming in and then going out.

3 If you want to, you can place your hands on your abdomen, to feel the movement of the breath as it moves in your body, right here under your hands (you can also silently say "in" as the breath moves all the way in, and then "out" as the breath moves back out.

4 If at any point, you notice that your mind has wandered away, remember that this is not a mistake or a problem – it is bound to happen and is what minds are designed to do. Just gently settle the attention back to noticing the breath and to the sensations of the waves of the breath, flowing in and out of your body.

Mike worked very long hours and often felt stressed. Recently, he had been feeling more tired than usual. He went to his doctor, who decided to refer him for tests at his local hospital. Now, on top of the physical symptoms Mike was adding all sorts of thoughts and worries, especially about the tests at the hospital.

Mike decided to try a grounding practice (see below) a few times a day for a few days. He found that if he really focused on feeling his feet on the floor, it helped him feel steadier, calmer and more balanced. He was surprised at how helpful something so simple could be. Encouraged by this, he decided to add the Physical Barometer (see page 171), which he had read about in a book by Bartley, on his journey on the train to and from work each day.

Mike found he could use these practices when he went to the hospital for his tests and as he waited for the results. He could return to feeling his feet on the floor as often as he needed and as a result he felt more "grounded" and here, in this moment and this place. He monitored his barometer with gentle curiosity and this helped him manage all the uncertainty involved in waiting for results and coping with the diagnosis. He realized that whether he worried or not, it wouldn't change the outcome of the tests, but he could change how he felt *now*. Learning to bring curiosity and friendliness to his experience felt very different from allowing the frustration and fear escalate in his mind and body. He saw that he could choose to take care of himself in this difficult situation he was dealing with.

Grounding Practice

You can do this practice standing, walking or sitting. You can also practise it at night, by bringing awareness to the contact of your body with the bed.

- Moving the attention to feeling your feet on the ground, explore all the detailed sensations in your toes, the balls of your feet, and in your heels.
- Bring your attention to the experience of texture (maybe socks or shoes), of contact (wherever you feel it), and of the weight of your legs and feet.

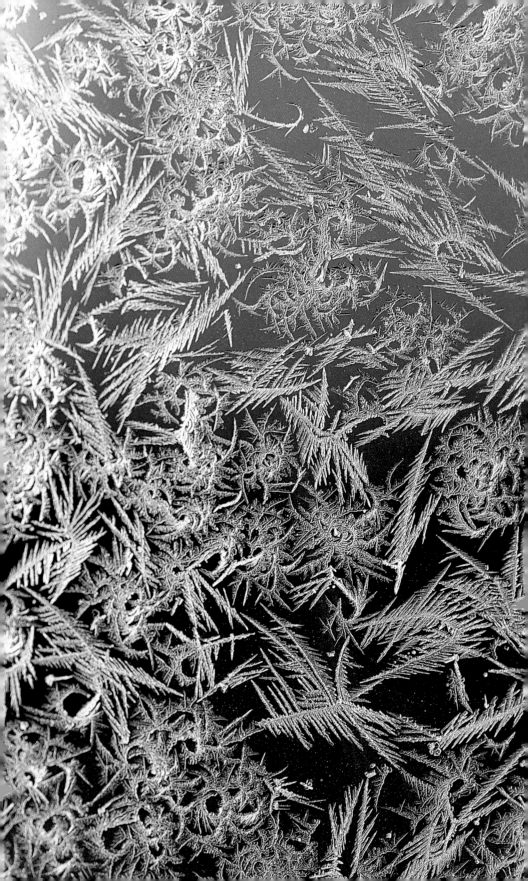

Exercise: The Physical Barometer

If you have seen an old fashioned barometer, you will know that you gently tap on the glass front and wait for the needle to respond. Depending on which way the needle moves, it is possible to forecast the weather. We can use our bodies in a similar way to give us sensitive information about the emotional "weather" arising for us. This exercise takes only a few minutes.

1 Choose some part of the trunk of your body to focus on – such as the chest area or the abdomen, or somewhere between the two – that for you is especially sensitive to stress, tension and difficulty.

2 Once you have found the place, it can be your "physical barometer". Choosing to tune into it regularly, you may discover different sensations at different times. When you are under pressure, feeling anxious, agitated or frustrated, you may notice sensations of tension, tightness, shakiness or discomfort. The intensity of these sensations varies depending on the level of your difficulty. Explore these sensations gently and with friendly interest.

3 As you practise this, you can learn to become aware of quite subtle sensations. They may signal that something is brewing for you, long before you are aware of this in your mind.

Dealing with a Diagnosis

Many of us have been or will be diagnosed with a physical health condition during our lifetime, and hearing the diagnosis may feel like a very significant moment in our life. Our situation may not have actually changed at all, but a lot of people say that it felt like everything changed when they received a diagnosis. Of course the diagnosis itself may well affect the degree of this experience. But who we are, our past experience, our understanding, our family history, lifestyle and aspirations will also add meaning to the news of the diagnosis.

Often the diagnosis can bring many more questions and perhaps images of how the future will be, based perhaps on only limited knowledge. There is often a great deal of uncertainty about the future and, in an attempt to manage this, the mind may become very active, planning for all eventualities. In these moments of wondering, worrying and planning, our mind is in the uncertain landscape of the future and we are actually not here with what is our present-moment experience.

It would be naive to think that we can always be with our experience just in this moment and ignoring the future. We may need to make plans to manage and respond to our illness. However, mindfulness can help us see the plans for what they are and that we are choosing to spend time planning. When the planning has been done we can choose to return to this moment. The Hot Air Balloon exercise, opposite, can help you see your current experience more clearly and from a broader perspective. In practising being open to what's here – the difficult and the pleasurable – and making room for it all to be as it is, you are learning to have a different kind of relationship with your experience, just as we explored in the Dancing with Difficulty exercise (see page 78).

Exercise: The Hot Air Balloon

This exercise helps us to explore the detail of our experience as it is just now. As you do it, include what is actually here in your experience in this moment, and try to resist the temptation to include things from your past or what may come to happen in the future. Bringing the image of a hot air balloon to mind (sitting on the ground with its sandbags attached to the large basket, the balloon inflated ready for flight), ask yourself what are the aspects of your experience today that are pulling you down like the sandbags on the air balloon?

- Do you have any physical pain or discomfort? Are you experiencing difficulties with mobility? Are there any challenges with managing everyday activities in life? Do you feel fatigue or tiredness?
- Are you experiencing worrying or gloomy thoughts about the future? Maybe memories are playing in your mind or perhaps you are longing for how things were in the past? Perhaps you are trying to make sense of why this has happened to you? Are you criticizing or judging yourself about how you are managing now?
- Do you feel anger, resentment, sadness or frustration about having this condition?
- Are you aware of other "sandbags"?

- Now spend time identifying the aspects of your experience – here, right now – that lift or support you. These, like the hot air in the balloon, can help you to feel lighter and more energized. They may be: things you enjoy; ways you can care for yourself; support you have from others in your life; things that you value in your life; activities that help you feel a sense of achievement and control, and that are available today; experiences of comfort and pleasure in your body in this moment; what your senses are telling you as you see, hear, taste, smell and feel the experiences that are here.
- Think of ways that you can release the sandbags or increase the experiences that lift you right now?

Becoming a Patient

It can feel as if there is a big shift in how we and other people see us when we have been diagnosed with a condition. Sometimes people with certain conditions are even referred to as "sufferers". We may find ourselves in the role of patients, with a schedule of hospital appointments, tests and medical investigations, having to deal with health professionals and waiting rooms in hospitals and clinics. As we rely on others' knowledge and expertise, we may feel we have less control over decisions in our life.

The medical system can invite us to focus on finding a cure and getting rid of our illness completely, sometimes raising expectations of this being possible. When we are lucky, treatment *can* make our symptoms go away. But in many cases there is no complete solution and the treatment itself may be a significant source of difficulty.

The Benefits of Mindfulness

We have seen that by being more mindful we can live in the present moment. We can learn to cope with what is actually happening when we are ill and reduce the impact of the second "arrows" that our thoughts, emotions, behaviours and reactive body can create.

Our illness, whether temporary or long-term, is here and is having its effect. We may not be able to change the condition itself in this moment, but its effect on us can be significantly influenced through mindful awareness. Regular mindfulness practice allows us to turn toward what's here in our mind and our body. We can begin to build trust in ourselves to be with, and manage, difficulty as it appears. We can find a steady place where we can see that there is also plenty to appreciate and enjoy in life, even if we are ill. We can bring an attitude of friendly interest and non-judgmental support for ourselves, learning to care for ourselves as we would for a good friend, and learning to choose skilful ways to respond and live our lives fully alongside our illness.

Further Exercises

Mountain Meditation

This exercise can help you to find the mountain's steadiness in yourself, despite the "weather" of your situation.

- Come to sit, or stand, in a balanced and dignified position with your feet (and knees if you are sitting on the floor) firmly connected with the ground, feeling the sensations of this.
- Notice your whole body here, tall and dignified, your spine long and lifting up from the steady base of your feet on the ground. The crown of your head is lifting gently upward.
- Come now to notice the breath movements in your body for a few minutes – the "aliveness" of this breath being breathed in and out.
- Now, if you choose to, bring to your mind the image of a mountain – perhaps one you know well, or one you have seen in pictures, or one you can imagine.
- Allow your mind to explore this image for a few moments. Notice the mountain's vast base where it connects with and is rooted to the earth. Explore the shape of its slopes and peak.
- Maybe notice, as you sit (or stand) here now that there are some of these qualities about your own experience. Perhaps feel your own "mountainness" as you sit (or stand) steadily here, still and magnificent.
- Realize that all mountains exist, still and rooted throughout the year as the seasons pass by. The mountain is heated by hot sun, frozen by snow and ice, buffeted by strong winds and drenched by rain. The mountain stays still, resilient, dignified and unchanged by the activity around it.
- Feel your "mountainess" as experiences come and go, finding stability and rootedness even when things are stormy.
- Come again to feel the sensations of your body here, seeing the place you are in. Can you sense the mountain's qualities in yourself as you continue with the activities in your day?

Guided Body Scan for Children

This works best if you adapt it for your child using a gentle and interested tone of voice. Start by making yourselves comfortable, lying down or sitting.

"Let yourself just settle and get comfortable. You can shut your eyes if you wish.

Now bring your attention to all the places in your body where you can feel your body touching the bed [or rug, chair and so on] ... the backs of your heels ... backs of your legs ... your bottom ... your back ... your arms ... shoulders ... and head ...

And now ... without trying to breathe in any special way, just notice that your breath is gently moving your body up and down ... noticing the places in your body where you can feel your breath ... [adjusting your pacing to suit]

Now moving your attention down to your feet [you might touch the feet area to help the child focus their attention here] *... notice your feet ... perhaps you can feel your feet against the bed? ... maybe you can feel the blanket over you? ...*

Now shifting your attention to your legs ... all the way from your ankles up to the tops of your legs ... can you feel how heavy your legs are against the bed? Perhaps you can feel the weight of your blanket over your legs? ...

Now your back ... feel your back against the bed ... feel your breath moving against your back ...

Now move your attention to the front of your body ... your tummy and your chest ... if you want to, you can put one hand on your tummy and one hand on your chest and feel your body move up and down as you breathe ...

Now your arms ... feel your arms and hands moving up and down on your tummy or chest as you breathe ... feel the weight of your arms on your body ... notice if your arms are warm or cold ... maybe they're different in different parts? ...

Now pay attention to your head, feeling the weight of your head on the pillow.

Pretend you can breathe all through your body down to your toes as you breathe in ... and as you breathe out, all the way back up to your head, nose and mouth. Now you have given attention to all your body, just notice what that feels like.

Further Resources

NOTE ON MINDFULNESS-BASED COGNITIVE THERAPY

As outlined in Chapter 1, Mindfulness-Based Cognitive Therapy (MBCT), developed by Zindel Segal, Mark Williams and John Teasdale, is specifically for people who are currently well but have a history of recurrent depression. The approach has been researched and has been found to approximately halve the likelihood of relapse into depression – a similar success rate to anti-depressant medications. The National Institute of Clinical Excellence (NICE) in the UK recommends MBCT as the treatment of choice for relapse prevention in those with a history of three or more episodes of depression. Willem Kuyken (see page 17) has also been carrying out research comparing MBCT and anti-depressant medication, and early findings suggest MBCT may be at least as effective as anti-depressants.

There is also no conflict between mindfulness classes and anti-depressant medication, so it is possible to explore mindfulness as a way of understanding and responding to your depression while still supported by anti-depressants.

WEBSITES

The websites listed opposite offer:

- useful information about mindfulness
- information about mindfulness classes and courses with experienced teachers
- mindfulness practice CDs and books

Be Mindful
http://www.bemindful.co.uk/learn/find_a_course

Be Mindful Australia
http://bemindful.com.au

Breathworks
http://breathworks-mindfulness.org.uk

Center for Mindfulness in Medicine, Health Care, and Society, University of
Massachusetts Medical School, Worcester, Massachusetts, USA
http://www.umassmed.edu/cfm

Centre for Mindfulness Research and Practice, School of Psychology, Bangor
University, North Wales, UK
http://www.bangor.ac.uk/mindfulness

Developing Mindfulness (a network for people interested in working with
children, adolescents and parents)
http://www.developingmindfulness.ning.org

Mindfulness Scotland
http://www.mindfulnessscotland.org.uk

Mood Disorders Centre, Exeter University, Exeter, UK
http://www.exeter.ac.uk/mooddisorders/aboutus

Oxford Centre for Mindfulness, Oxford, UK
http://oxfordmindfulness.org

Index

Acknowledgments

I want to offer my sincere thanks to all my mindfulness teachers. My continued developing mindfulness practice, understanding and commitment to this work is directly due to the enormous wisdom and support of Jon Kabat-Zinn, Mark Williams, Melissa Blacker, Pam Erdmann, Ferris Urbanowski, Cindy Cooper and David Rynick. Thank you too to John and Leah for their support, building me a creative space to write and having patience when writing took me away from spending time with them. Thank you too to my co-authors, Eluned and Vanessa, with whom it has been a real pleasure to work with on this book. Trish Bartley, Elaine Weatherly-Jones, Mariel Jones and others in the CMRP teaching team offered crucial inspiration and guidance during development of the book and Illness chapter especially. Last, and by no means least, thank you to Sandra Rigby, Fiona Robertson, Suzanne Tuhrim, Jane McIntosh and the rest of the Duncan Baird team for their enthusiasm and wisdom as the book has taken shape.

PICTURE CREDITS

The publisher would like to thank the following people, museums and photographic libraries for permission to reproduce their material. Every care has been taken to trace copyright holders. However, if we have omitted anyone we apologize and will, if informed, make corrections to any future edition.

Key: Getty=Getty Images, DBP=Duncan Baird Publishers, London

Page 5–9 teekaygee/Shutterstock; **11** CLM/Shutterstock; **15–16** Image Werks/Corbis; **20** Jules Selmes/ DBP; **21** teekaygee/Shutterstock; **25–6** CLM/Shutterstock; **27** Darrell Gulin/Corbis; **31–8** Fotosav/ Shutterstock; **39** Pat O'Hara/Corbis; **40** teekaygee/Shutterstock; **43** Josh Westrich/Corbis; **44** teekaygee/ Shutterstock; **47–50** Simon Smith & Toby Scott/DBP; **53** MECKY/Getty; **55–60** Jules Selmes/DBP; **63** Charriau Pierre/Getty; **65–9** Jules Selmes/DBP; **71–3** teekaygee/Shutterstock; **78** Jules Selmes/DBP; **81** Nigel Blythe/Robert Harding World Imagery/Corbis; **89** Giorgio Fochesato/Getty; **90** teekaygee/ Shutterstock; **93–4** Nigel Blythe/Robert Harding World Imagery/Corbis; **96** Image Werks/Corbis; **99** George Doyle/Getty; **101** Serp/Shutterstock; **105** teekaygee/Shutterstock; **109** George Doyle/Getty; **111** Martin Ruegner/Getty; **113** Image Werks/Corbis; **115** Stockbyte/Getty; **119** Zac Macaulay/Getty; **124** Nils Hendrik Mueller/Getty; **126** Image Werks/Corbis; **127** Jules Selmes/DBP; **131** PIER/Getty; **133** Image Werks/Corbis; **135** PIER/Getty; **136** BestPhotoByMonikaGniot/Shutterstock; **138** Lauren Burke/Getty; **145** Gyro Photography/amanaimages/Corbis; **148** Image Werks/Corbis; **151** Gyro Photography/amanaimages/Corbis; **152** Andy Crawford/Getty; **153** Jules Selmes/DBP; **154** Image Werks/ Corbis; **155** Jules Selmes/DBP; **157** Mark Scoggins/Getty; **161** Gerolf Kalt/Corbis; **164** teekaygee/ Shutterstock; **167** Charles C. Place/Getty; **168** Jules Selmes/DBP; **170** Ocean/Corbis; **171** Jules Selmes/ DBP; **173–4** Gerolf Kalt/Corbis.

SOLUTION TO NINE-STAR PUZZLE ON PAGE 121

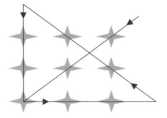